THE END
OF PROCRASTINATION

HOW TO STOP POSTPONING AND LIVE A FULFILLED LIFE

ST. MARTIN'S ESSENTIALS

NEW YORK

PETR LUDWIG
ADELA SCHICKER

THE
END
OF
PRO
CRASTI
NATION

PROCRASTINATION =
PUTTING THINGS OFF
INTENTIONALLY OR
HABITUALLY

www.stmartins.com

The Library of Congress Cataloging-in-Publication Data is available upon request.

ISBN 978-1-250-30805-4 (trade paperback)
ISBN 978-1-250-30806-1 (ebook)

Our books may be purchased in bulk for promotional, educational, or business use. Please contact your local bookseller or the Macmillan Corporate and Premium Sales Department at 1-800-221-7945, extension 5442, or by email at MacmillanSpecialMarkets@macmillan.com.

Originally published in the Czech Republic by Jan Melvil Publishing under the title *Konec prokrastinace*

First U.S. Edition: December 2018

10 9 8 7 6 5 4 3 2 1

Hope is not the conviction that something will turn out well but the certainty that something has meaning, regardless of how it turns out.

—V. Havel

Contents

THE TABLE OF CONTENTS ILLUSTRATED

INTRINSIC MOTIVATION
SELF-CONTROL
PRODUCTIVITY AND EFFECTIVENESS
HAPPINESS
FLOW
HABITS

Author's Preface

Approximately ten years ago, I was convinced my life was over. During playing sports, my brain had unexpectedly malfunctioned, resulting in a medical condition where the right side of my body was completely paralyzed.

I was overcome by fear and a feeling of powerlessness, yet at the same time I felt an eerie sense of peace. As I lay in bed, my entire life flashed before my eyes. At one point, it seemed as if I was travelling down a tunnel towards a light: it was just like in the movies. I began summing up my life, thinking about my failures and accomplishments. I slowly came to grips with the fact that I was dying.

But fortunately, as it turned out, I had been mistaken. A few days later, everything was slowly getting back to normal, luckily without any sign of long-term harm; I had survived a close encounter with death. It was the most powerful experience I have ever had in my life. Later, so that I would never forget that moment, I jotted down the following thought to myself:

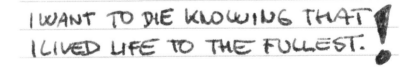

I WANT TO DIE KNOWING THAT I LIVED LIFE TO THE FULLEST!

When I set off fulfilling this resolution, I discovered that I would have to defeat a very fierce enemy: procrastination.

So, a few friends and I decided to get to the bottom of why we tended to put things off and why we were so indecisive and ineffective. We soon discovered that a large number of scientific studies had been conducted on these very same issues in recent years. Based on these studies, we put together a practical toolkit for fighting procrastination.

Once we realized that these methods worked for us, we decided that it would be beneficial to share them with as many people as possible. We began offering training courses for the public as well as lectures for university students. Helping other people better utilize their time and potential brought meaning to our lives.

I was inspired to create even better tools for fighting procrastination through my consulting practice. Over the course of years, I visited a large number of companies around the globe. I had the opportunity to consult with their executives about how to motivate workers and how to increase employee effectiveness and happiness at work. In the past decade, tens of thousand people have attended our training courses. Based on clients' experiences and their feedback, we began to improve our tools into their present form.

At some point my future publisher approached me and asked if I wanted to write a book. "What a great challenge," was my first thought; it also seemed like an exceptional way to further test the methods I teach.

But would I procrastinate or not procrastinate when it actually came to writing a book about procrastination?

Since I am an extrovert who is used to working with people—I teach and provide counseling—writing this book became one of the greatest challenges of my life. In order not to put off writing, a typically introverted activity and therefore not something I was used to doing, I had to deploy all my anti-procrastination weapons at full strength.

Since you are holding this book in your hands, it means I was successful. I hope you enjoy reading it, and I wish you all the best in your fight against procrastination. You will gradually succeed; I am sure of it.

Petr Ludwig

INTRODUCTION

WHAT IS PROCRASTINATION AND WHY FIGHT IT?

PRO-CRASTINUS
= (LAT.) BELONGING TO TOMORROW

PROCRASTINATION
= PUTTING THINGS OFF INTENTIONALLY OR HABITUALLY

If you have ever had trouble persuading yourself to do things you should do or would like to do, you have experienced procrastination. When you procrastinate, instead of working on important meaningful tasks, you find yourself performing trivial activities.

If you are a typical procrastinator, perhaps you spend an excessive amount of time hitting the snooze button, watching TV, playing video games, checking Facebook, eating (even when you are not hungry), obsessively cleaning, pacing back and forth through the office, or maybe just sitting and staring at a wall. Afterwards, you feel powerless and are overcome with feelings of guilt and frustration. Once again, you end up doing nothing. Sound familiar?

But careful now. Procrastination isn't pure **laziness**. Lazy people simply don't do anything and are just fine with it. Procrastinators, however, have the desire to actually do something but can't force themselves to start. They truly want to fulfill their obligations but just can't figure out how.

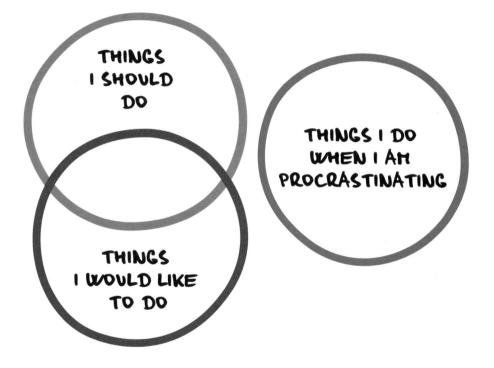

Don't confuse procrastination with **relaxation** either. Relaxing recharges you with energy. In stark contrast, procrastinating drains it from you. The less energy you have, the greater the chances of you putting off your responsibilities are, and, once more, you will accomplish nothing.

People often love leaving things to the last minute too. They justify their actions by claiming that they work better under pressure. However, the opposite is true.[1] Putting things off until the very last moment creates fertile ground for stress, guilt, and ineffectiveness. The old saying *"Don't put off till tomorrow what you can do today"* really hits the nail on the head.

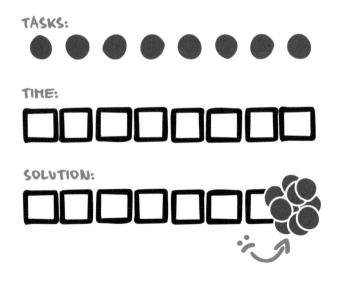

A History of Putting Things Off

Since the dawn of time, people have suffered from procrastination. As the classic Greek poet Hesiod commented on this problem in his poem *Works and Days:*[2]

> *Do not postpone for tomorrow*
> *or the day after tomorrow;*
> *barns are not filled by those who postpone*
> *and waste time in aimlessness.*
> *Work prospers with care;*
> *he who postpones wrestles with ruin.*

Those who postpone and waste time in aimlessness—this is how you could describe today's *procrastinator.*

Seneca, the Roman philosopher, also warned: *"While we waste our time hesitating and postponing, life is slipping away."* This quotation reveals the main reason why learning to overcome procrastination is so important.

Procrastination is one of the main barriers blocking you from living life to its fullest. Recent studies have shown that people don't regret the things they have done but the things they haven't done.[3] Feelings of regret and guilt resulting from missed opportunities tend to stay with people much longer.

When you procrastinate, you waste time that you could be investing into something meaningful. If you can overcome this fierce enemy, you will be able to accomplish more and in doing so better utilize potential life offers.

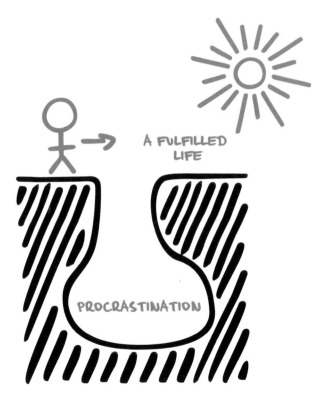

Today's Age of Decision Paralysis

So what's the situation with procrastination like today? Today's world plays into the hands of procrastinating. And learning how to overcome it is therefore one of the most important skills you can learn in this day and age.

In the last one hundred years the average human lifespan has more than doubled.[4] Infant mortality is a tenth of what it was a century ago.[5] Every morning, we wake up in a world where there is less violence and military conflict than in any other time in history.[6] Thanks to the Internet, almost all human knowledge is available to us with just a few clicks. There are practically no limits on travel; you can go nearly anywhere in the world. Knowing another language enables people to understand and be understood in foreign countries. The cell phone you carry around in your pocket is more powerful than the best supercomputers were twenty years ago.[7]

The amount of opportunities that today's world offers is staggering. Imagine the extent of these opportunities as if it was the space in between an open pair of scissors. The more opportunities you have, the wider this imaginary pair of scissors—*the scissors of potential*—opens. Today, they are open wider than they have ever been in history.

Modern society idolizes individual liberty and the belief that the freer people are, the happier they will be. According to this theory, every time the scissors of potential open a bit further, you should be happier and happier. So then why aren't people today significantly happier than in the past?[8] Why is it so problematic that the scissors of potential are constantly opening wider?

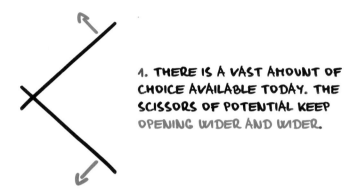

1. THERE IS A VAST AMOUNT OF CHOICE AVAILABLE TODAY. THE SCISSORS OF POTENTIAL KEEP OPENING WIDER AND WIDER.

More opportunities make for more choices—and an unexpected problem: the more choices there are, the harder it is to make a decision.[9] *Decision paralysis* sets in. Considering each and every option available to you consumes so much energy that you may find yourself unable to make any decision at all.[10] When this happens, you postpone making decisions and subsequently end up putting off actions. You are procrastinating.

The more complicated comparing the options is, the greater is our tendency to put off making a decision.[11] Moreover, if you have many choices available, it is likely that even if you do pick one, you will end up regretting your decision.[12] You might imagine what it would have been like if you had chosen the other way around. You will easily see the short-comings of what you have chosen.

Do you know that feeling when you have something to do, but you don't do it anyway? Can you recall the last time you put off doing some-thing or making a decision? Have you ever been unable to choose from the choices before you? What kind of feelings did you have in these situations?

When decision paralysis increases, it lends itself to increasing pro-crastination.[13] Putting things off can then lower your productivity to the point that it is only a fraction of what it could be. Realizing that you are not living up to your potential can lead to guilt and frustration.

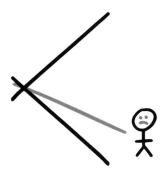

2. BEING PRESENTED WITH TOO MANY CHOICES LEADS TO DECISION PARALYSIS. IT BECOMES A SOURCE OF PROCRASTINATION AND FRUSTRATION THAT PREVENTS YOU FROM LIVING UP TO YOUR POTENTIAL.

At its core, this book is a set of simple tools that will help you utilize your potential much better on a daily basis. Using them requires a few minutes out of a day, but in the end, you will gain several extra hours of productive time.

With our tools, you can overcome the imperfections that have evolved in the human brain. They will help you overcome both inherent and learned tendencies to be ineffective. One side effect of battling procrastination is that the reward center of the brain will be more frequently activated.[14] This means you will experience more positive emotions.

How did you feel the last time you really lived a day to the fullest? When was that? In this book, you will find out why living up to your potential on a daily basis is the most effective path to long-term happiness.

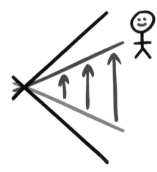

3. SIMPLE TOOLS CAN BOOST YOUR EFFECTIVENESS. LIVING UP TO YOUR POTENTIAL LEADS TO HAPPINESS.

What Is the Most Effective Way to Get Information?

Not only does this book reveal the reasons why people procrastinate, but it will also arm you with the weapons to help defeat this powerful foe. But upon what foundation should we build our knowledge about personal development?

Today, there are ten times more scientific studies on procrastination than there were a decade ago.[15] But in today's world, valuable facts are often washed away in a flood of poor-quality information. It is becoming more and more important to know your way around in today's information age. Will Rogers once said: *"Our problem isn't that we know too little. Our problem is that much of what we do know isn't true."*

There are thousands of personal development how-to guides, articles, and books out there today. Not long ago, I counted three hundred such titles at just one tiny bookstore. And there are thousands more available online. The mass availability of information has many risks.

The first problem is that **the information available is highly chaotic** and frequently of poor quality. Different books advise you to take contrasting approaches. Some recommend you reward yourself every time you accomplish a task; others advise you not to reward yourself under any circumstance. Some guides are based on unconfirmed claims or on the experience of just one individual, which can hardly be applied to everyone's situation. Many books contain myths and half-truths that have been passed on from author to author.

Perhaps you've heard this statement before: *University researchers conducted a study of the relationship between people's goals and their accomplishments. They asked their subjects if they were able to write down specific goals they have in life, and, if in the future, they would be willing to share information about their income. Only 3 percent of participants were able to write down their goals. Several years later, the researchers tracked down the participants and discovered that the 3 percent of participants that had been capable of writing down their goals had made more money than the remaining 97 percent of study participants combined.* The problem with this claim is that no such research has ever been done.[16] It is the product of someone's imagination, an urban legend. Personal development books are full of myths just like this.

The sheer volume of information available causes another problem: **it amplifies decision paralysis**. The more sources of information you have, the harder it is to pick just one and trust it. What information should you base important life decisions on? How do you know what you can really trust?

In recent years, many studies have been conducted at top universities around the world focusing on motivation, decision-making, and effectiveness. The findings of these studies, however, often get lost in today's information chaos. And this is where the third problem comes in: **there is a gap between what science knows and what people do**.

AVAILABLE INFORMATION:

1. IT'S CHAOTIC AND FULL OF MYTHS AND HALF-TRUTHS.

2. DECISION PARALYSIS HAS SET IN. YOU DON'T KNOW WHAT TO BELIEVE OR WHAT TO BASE YOUR DECISIONS ON.

3. THERE IS A GAP BETWEEN WHAT SCIENCE KNOWS AND WHAT PEOPLE DO.

The goal of this book is to help bridge this information gap. To help you save time, we have processed the latest research and connected the dots between key findings. Finally, using all of this information, we have created a set of *illustrated models*. They are simple diagrams that will help you quickly understand how things work.

Philosopher Arthur Schopenhauer once said: *"Nothing is more difficult than to express important ideas so that everyone understands them."* Therefore, to improve understanding we use these illustrated models.

The part of the brain which processes images and visual information is called the *visual cortex*. Since it is one of the most developed parts of the human brain,[17] one diagram can tell you more than several pages of text. It can also better describe complex relationships and connections. You can also refer to the illustrations when you forget what a certain concept is all about and need to quickly jog your memory.

Thanks to this, illustrated models are much more effective for transferring information than plain linear text. We call this method of working with information *know-how design*; for us it is an easy way to transfer core knowledge to you.

Sometimes we intentionally redefine *terms* so that readers are sure what we mean by the words we use. It's a good idea to start using the word **procrastination** instead of the terms laziness or putting things off. It provides a much more accurate description of your situation. By giving the right name to your problem it's easier to find the solution.

KNOW-HOW DESIGN:

1. IN TODAY'S AGE OF INFORMATION OVERLOAD, WE HAVE PICKED OUT THE BEST INFORMATION AVAILABLE.

2. WE HAVE CONNECTED THE DOTS BETWEEN FINDINGS.

3. FINALLY, WE HAVE CREATED SIMPLE MODELS CAPABLE OF QUICKLY EXPLAINING HOW THINGS WORK.

Since many important ideas have been eloquently formulated by people before us, we also make use of quotes. They are simple, to-the-point, and capable of providing elegant summaries.

So let's get going. How do motivation, effectiveness, and happiness really work? How can you overcome procrastination? How can you make long-term, measurable changes in your life?

A System of Personal Development

Besides the introduction and conclusion, this book is divided into four relatively independent sections.

The first section explains how **motivation** works and contains a toolkit that can help you create a *Personal vision*. This is a tool that will help you find and maintain long-term intrinsic motivation.

The second section focuses on **discipline**, or the skill of effectively living up to your vision through performing certain key activities and sticking to daily habits. It contains clear methods for fighting procrastination, tools for task and time management, and tools for learning positive habits and getting rid of negative ones.

The third section is focused on the **outcomes** of your actions and describes methods for maintaining happiness. Practical tools will help you gain greater emotional stability; you will learn how to become more resistant to failures and negative external influences.

The fourth and final topic this book covers is **objectivity**—the ability to see through the false perceptions you have of both the world around you and of yourself. Only once you identify your flaws can you begin fixing them.

PERSONAL DEVELOPMENT

1. MOTIVATION
2. DISCIPLINE
3. OUTCOMES
4. OBJECTIVITY

Motivation

We were all born and unfortunately at some point will all die too. The time we spend on Earth is both limited and finite. In light of these facts, **time** is the most valuable commodity you have in life. It's not money; unlike time, you can borrow it, save, or earn more. You can't do that with time. Every single second you waste is gone forever.

In a commencement speech given to students at Stanford University, Steve Jobs eloquently expressed the finality of life: *"Remembering that I'll be dead soon is the most important tool I've ever encountered to help me make the big choices in life. Because almost everything—all external expectations, all pride, all fear of embarrassment or failure—these things just fall away in the face of death, leaving only what is truly important. Remembering that you are going to die is the best way I know to avoid the trap of thinking you have something to lose."*

The mere realization that life is finite leads people to begin managing their time more carefully. It makes you start thinking about how you would ideally like to spend your time on Earth. It makes you start looking for a **personal vision**.

PERSONAL VISION

THE FUTURE

1. MOTIVATION:

THE PRESENT

Your vision, once established, will become the most effective motivation imaginable and will pull you forward in life like a strong magnet. It will help you do things you see as being truly meaningful today, and at the same time draw you towards your ideal future.

Discipline

There are two sides to everyday discipline: *productivity* and *effectiveness*. There are only 24 hours in a day—no more, no less. Subtract the time you spend sleeping, and what you have left is potential productive time.

Productivity is an expression of what percent of your waking time you spend doing meaningful things, the activities that contribute to fulfilling your personal vision. Regular rest, time management, and positive habits can significantly boost your productivity.

Effectiveness determines whether the things you spend your time doing are key activities or not, in other words, those activities that move you forward as quickly as possible in life. Being able to determine priorities, split up tasks, and delegate responsibilities is crucial for improving personal effectiveness.

ONE DAY (24 HRS):

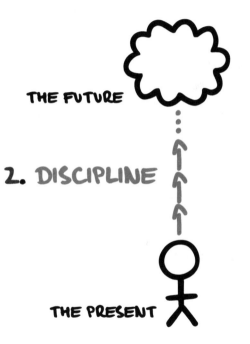

THE FUTURE

2. DISCIPLINE

THE PRESENT

Imagine your vision as a path. Productivity is an expression of how long you spend travelling on this path per day. Effectiveness determines whether you are taking the biggest steps you can. **Discipline** is therefore your overall ability to take specific actions that lead to the fulfillment of your personal vision.

Outcomes

As the old Japanese proverb goes: *"Vision without action is a daydream. Action without vision is a nightmare."* This saying addresses two major problems people have in life. Many people have ideas about what they would like to do, yet don't act on them. On the other hand, there are those who do things, yet see no purpose in their actions. Ideally, you need both; vision and action. When you successfully combine the two, you will get the *emotional* and *material outcomes.*

Emotional outcomes are related to the flooding of your brain with *dopamine*[18], a neurotransmitter that, when released, makes you happy.

Material outcomes are the concrete results of your actions—the fruits of your labor.

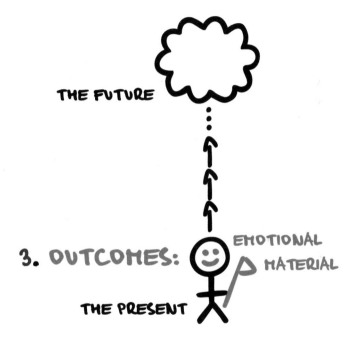

THE FUTURE

3. OUTCOMES:

EMOTIONAL
MATERIAL

THE PRESENT

Objectivity

The last important piece of our personal development system is improving objectivity. Anders Breivik, who shot 69 people to death on the Norwegian island of Utøya, was most likely very highly motivated and disciplined; his actions even resulted in emotional and material outcomes. This extreme case however demonstrates the lengths things can go to when someone does not have their objectivity under control.

The ability to increase your objectivity is an important tool you can use to counter your intuition when it fails you. By reducing your biases, you will be able to see how things work in reality more clearly. In order to increase your objectivity, you need to get feedback on your behavior, ideas, and actions. As our brains often have the tendency to believe things that are not true in reality, you need to constantly search out areas in your thinking that lack objectivity.

As Nobel laureate Bertrand Russell, one of the most important mathematicians and philosophers of the twentieth century, once stated: *"The fundamental cause of the trouble is that in the modern world the stupid are cocksure while the intelligent are full of doubt."*

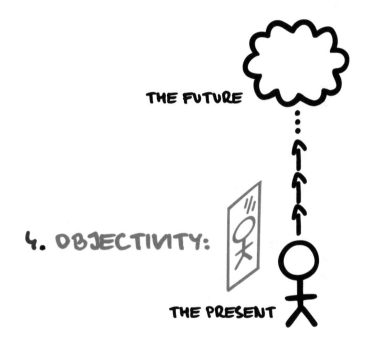

4. OBJECTIVITY:

Chapter Recap: Introduction

Procrastination is not pure laziness; it is the inability to persuade yourself to do the things you should or would like to do.

If we look back into history, we find that people have been putting off their responsibilities since the dawn of time.

Today's world plays into the hands of procrastinating more and more, and therefore you need to begin learning how to fight it.

The extent of opportunities available to you today is unlike anything that has ever existed in the past. **The scissors of potential** are open as wide as they have ever been.

Greater choice does not necessarily mean more happiness. Just the opposite is often true, as it is the cause of **decision paralysis**.

When you are paralyzed, you hesitate and put things off even more. You end up wasting time and as a result experience unpleasant emotions.

Simple tools exist that can help you overcome paralysis and procrastination.

When you live up to your potential, the reward center of your brain is more frequently activated, releasing **dopamine** and resulting in the experience of positive emotions.

Long-term happiness can be achieved by learning how to live every day meaningfully and to the fullest.

Procrastination can be overcome once you improve your **motivation**, **discipline**, **outcomes**, and **objectivity**.

Before we examine motivation in more detail, try rating yourself in these four key areas on a scale of 1 to 10 (1 being the worst, 10 the best).

How is your overall **motivation**? What about your **discipline**—your productivity and effectiveness? How would you rate your **outcomes**—happiness and the real results of your work? And how would you rate your attempts at being **objective**?

At the end of each chapter, you will make similar self-assessments. In the future, you will be able to return to them and observe your progress.

MOTIVATION

HOW TO GET MOTIVATED AND STAY THAT WAY

When I was in Denmark, I had the opportunity to spend some time at the offices of Novo Nordisk. This company, which employs more than 30,000 people, is the world leader in insulin production with a global market share of more than fifty percent.[19]

Upon arrival, I immediately noticed that the people I met there seemed highly motivated and happy—from the receptionists and the cleaning women I met in the hall to the people working in drug development. Since Novo Nordisk is, after all, a pharmaceutical company, it occurred to me that they must put something "special" in their employees' drinks. Later, I had the chance to spend some time with company executives and ask them what they do to have such happy and motivated employees. The explanation I received was surprisingly simple. So, what is the secret to motivation?

In the real world there are **several types of motivation**; some do more harm than good. Therefore, you need to find the one that will benefit you the most. The right kind of motivation will make you procrastinate less, it will become what drives you every day, and it will lead you down the path to long-term happiness.

Extrinsic Motivation: The Carrot and the Stick

Not long ago, I had an appointment with a new client. After speaking with him for a bit, he began to describe how he had been feeling for the past few years. He confided in me that his life was lacking meaning. He had even thought about taking his life on several occasions. I asked him how much time he spent doing things that he truly wanted to do, and, in contrast, how much time he spent doing things he had to do—things that were expected of him. In our discussion, it slowly became clear that he was driven almost exclusively by *extrinsic motivation*.

What kind of feelings do you have when you must do something that has no meaning for you? How do you feel spending your time doing things you are obliged to do even though you don't want to do them?

Recent research has shown that doing meaningless activities is usually very unpleasant and de-motivating.[20] These types of tasks, such as learning a poem by heart in school or doing assignments at work in which you see no purpose, can be a real turnoff, so it is no wonder that people put them off.

Extrinsic motivators—**rewards and punishments**, the carrot and the stick—have been developed to force people into doing these types of things against their will. These external stimuli make you perform actions you would never consider on your own.

There are, however, several major drawbacks to extrinsic motivation. When people do things they don't want to do, they are less happy and their brains release less dopamine. This substance, besides influencing happiness, also impacts creativity, memory, and the ability to learn.[21] Another disadvantage is that the unhappiness that extrinsic motivation creates is socially contagious; people who suffer from discontent infect those around them.[22]

It was extrinsic motivation that kept serfs working the fields during feudalism, galley slaves rowing in Ancient Rome, and people working in the first factories during the Industrial Revolution. These jobs involved practically no creativity. In contrast, the vast majority of jobs people do today require a creative approach. We need to carefully think through problems; we often have to improvise and look for unconventional solutions.

Many studies have confirmed that using extrinsic motivation lowers performance in activities that require even a little brainwork and creativity.[23] It is irrelevant if motivation comes from the carrot or from the stick.[24] If you expect a reward and don't get it, it has a similar effect on your psyche as if you were punished.

The imaginary stick hanging over us often makes us despise what we have to do.[25] This stick may come in the form of mortgage payments that prevent people from quitting jobs they loathe, it might be parents picking out hobbies or college majors and forcing them on their children, or it could be the boss at work who gives his subordinates assignments without explaining why. Antipathy is a natural outcome of extrinsic stimuli and often causes procrastination to grow.

EXTRINSIC MOTIVATION:

EXTRINSIC MOTIVATION CAUSES YOU TO BE UNHAPPY;
THE BRAIN RELEASES LESS DOPAMINE, LOWERING YOUR
CREATIVITY AND NEGATIVELY AFFECTING YOUR LEARNING
ABILITIES. THE NEGATIVE EMOTIONS IT PRODUCES ARE
SOCIALLY CONTAGIOUS.

People accustomed to being extrinsically motivated stop being able to work independently. When the stick disappears, they can't get themselves motivated. School grades are a good example of an extrinsic motivator. Students, for example, get used to studying to receive grades, but once they graduate and this pressure disappears, they often stop educating themselves. Extrinsic motivation suppresses future initiative in people, and without the stick they aren't able to do hardly anything.

My client had been ruled by extrinsic motivation almost his entire life. Unhappiness, the inability to learn new things, and his literally murdered creativity led him to giving up on life.

The first good news in this chapter is that there is a way to get out of striking range of the stick: you can escape the trap of extrinsic motivation. But beware, however, as many motivational books and coaches can lead you into another trap. They often promote a cure in the form of *intrinsic goal-based motivation.*

Intrinsic Goal-Based Motivation: Joy That Doesn't Last

"Peter, think about what would make you happy. Picture those things in detail. Do you see a car? Imagine exactly what color it is, what brand, what kind of engine. Go to the showroom and get behind the wheel. . . . Take some paper and carefully write down all your wishes, and, ideally, find some pictures to match. Make sure to assign a deadline for fulfilling each one. Now hang it all up in a place where you can see it. These will be your

goals. These will be the things that are going to motivate you." This is how my first personal development coach worked. He motivated people by using their dreams and goals.

Over the course of my career, I met several people who have been nearly destroyed by this kind of motivation. As studies indicate, goal-based motivation can improve productivity, but it does not lead to long-term happiness.[26] Instead it contributes to unexpected frustration and a strange form of addiction, not unlike being hooked on cocaine.[27] Why is goal-based motivation so treacherous? What's behind it?

Goal setting involves the use of the *prefrontal cortex*,[28] the part of the brain that allows us to dream at night and which enables us to visualize things in our head that don't yet exist. The prefrontal cortex allows human beings, unlike other animals, to think about their own future.[29]

INTRINSIC GOAL-BASED MOTIVATION:

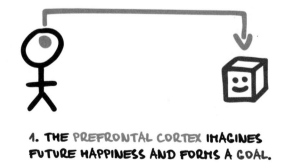

1. THE PREFRONTAL CORTEX IMAGINES FUTURE HAPPINESS AND FORMS A GOAL.

What would make you happy? The partner of your dreams and two healthy children? Finishing school or doubling your salary? What about a new house with a pool, or a month long vacation, or something else you've been dreaming of?

Just as the prefrontal cortex can vividly imagine your goals, it can also visualize the happiness you will feel once you achieve them.

Recall that goals truly are strong motivators. Unlike extrinsic motivation, people who are motivated by goals do things because they really want to. This makes them work with great intensity.

Since their present situation doesn't meet their expectations and desires, they aren't particularly happy. Because they still don't have that car, it drives them in life, and they have the feeling that something is missing; they are not happy with their present. This is why on the way to achieving their goal they don't often experience the benefits associated with increased dopamine levels: better brain function, greater creativity, and the ability to effectively learn new things.

Goals drive people forward, causing them to work hard, which means that sooner or later, they will indeed achieve them. And when that finally does happen, a one-time dose of dopamine is released, resulting in an intense emotion: a type of happiness we call the *emotion of joy*.[30] The problem is that what follows next is something the prefrontal cortex wasn't counting on. A phenomenon known as *hedonic adaptation* sets in.[31]

2. ON THE WAY TO YOUR GOAL YOU ARE NOT HAPPY BECAUSE YOU STILL HAVEN'T ACHIEVED IT.

Try to imagine what it was like passing a hard test in school or finishing a difficult project at work. Try to remember how you felt the last time you bought something you really wanted. What was your feeling immediately afterwards? Were your emotions just as strong two days later? How about after a week?

Hedonic adaptation causes people to unexpectedly get accustomed to their accomplished goals. A few minutes, hours or, at most, days upon reaching a goal, positive feelings tend to disappear. If you have ever bought a new car, perhaps you were surprised to find that after a week you were beginning to take your new vehicle almost for granted. After a few days, your emotions were incomparably weaker than immediately following your purchase.

3. UPON ACHIEVING A GOAL, THE TEMPORARY POSITIVE EMOTION OF JOY IS PRODUCED. DUE TO HEDONIC ADAPTATION, HOWEVER, YOU QUICKLY GET USED TO YOUR NEW ACCOMPLISHMENT, AND YOUR POSITIVE EMOTIONS QUICKLY DISAPPEAR.

Even if you reach the highest rung of the ladder, for example if you win the Nobel Prize or a gold medal in the Olympics, after a few weeks even these accomplishments will have hardly any effect on your happiness.[32] Soon enough, they will stop writing about you in the papers, and you will slowly fall into oblivion. Hedonic adaptation will have caught up with you once again.

One study measured how happy people felt after winning the lottery.[33] Simultaneously, researchers also studied how people who were recently paralyzed felt. The results indicated that just after one year both groups were almost comparably happy. You can adapt to things that at first you might not expect.

Some people are very envious of others. From the perspective of hedonic adaptation, however, envy is not very reasonable. Even if they are envious and do manage to get what they desire, hedonic adaptation will not allow them to feel happier. They would soon get used to having the things they had once craved.

Extensive studies on how money influences happiness have come to a clear conclusion: money affects happiness only to the point that it helps you secure basic needs for yourself and your family.[34] Beyond this point, more money barely affects your happiness.

A GRAPH OF HOW MONEY INFLUENCES HAPPINESS:

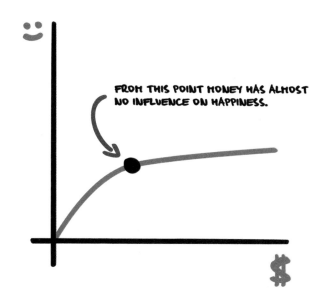

FROM THIS POINT MONEY HAS ALMOST NO INFLUENCE ON HAPPINESS.

The pitfall of the prefrontal cortex is that although it is exceptional at visualizing goals and the happiness you will feel once you achieve them, it cannot foresee the short lifespan of these positive emotions. The prefrontal cortex is unable to foresee hedonic adaptation.

If you are looking forward to getting a new car, your brain can imagine the joy you will feel when it is new, but it can't see any deeper into the future to realize that this joy is only temporary. This is one of the main reasons why we are often wrong when it comes to judging how happy we will be in the future.

But how do people motivated by goals react to hedonic adaptation? It's simple. Once they have reached the desired goal and their positive emotions have worn off, they set another, **even bigger goal**: "I guess the Audi didn't make me happy. But a Porsche will." And the chase begins all over. Once again, they aren't happy on the way to achieving this new goal because they still don't have it. They work and work, and perhaps they will get what they want again. Then they will experience the emotion of joy, but thanks to hedonic adaptation that feeling will once again soon disappear. And their reaction? They set another bigger goal. And the cycle repeats itself over and over.

The emotion of joy produced by achieving a goal affects the same part of the brain that is activated by a hit of cocaine.[35] Thus, joy can lead to what is called *arousal addictions*.[36] Addictions to pornography, video games, and adrenaline sports also belong in this same category.

4. YOU SET ANOTHER LARGER GOAL. THE CYCLE REPEATS ITSELF, AND YOU MAY BECOME A GOAL JUNKIE.

Adrenaline junkies have to jump off higher and higher cliffs and do more extreme things in order to experience the same rush. Pornography addicts have to watch increasingly more perverted videos to reach the same level of arousal. In the same way, people who are motivated by goals must constantly set their sights higher and higher. They become what we call *goal junkies*. They might have big houses and expensive cars as well as the positions they have always dreamed of, but at the same time they are capable of feeling only short bursts of happiness. They are often depressed; they have everything except long-term well-being.

The first good news I shared in this chapter was that you can escape from the stick of extrinsic motivation. The second piece of good news I have is that there is an alternative to intrinsic goal-based motivation. It is called *intrinsic journey-based motivation*, and it provides the benefits of the intensity of intrinsic motivation but at the same time avoids hedonic adaptation and thus can keep you happier in the present.

Intrinsic Journey-Based Motivation: Happiness Now

So what substance were they adding to people's drinks at Novo Nordisk? What was their secret? At my meetings with company executives, I discovered that the key to keeping employees highly motivated and happy is having a very strong company vision and values. Their purpose is to make the lives of people with diabetes better.[37]

I was told stories about the company that proved to me that their vision statement is not just an empty phrase. For example, my hosts told me about how, during the war, their company provided insulin to both sides for free, or how the NovoPen, a tool for painlessly injecting insulin, was invented. Nearly every employee, no matter their position in the company, can connect with the higher cause expressed in the company's vision: the idea of improving the lives of people with diabetes. When people see meaning in their actions, particularly when they actually want to perform these actions, one of the strongest forms of motivation arises: **intrinsic journey-based motivation**.

This type of motivation, the third one I discuss, is based on the concept of having a **personal vision**. Unlike chasing goals, a process that we know is affected by hedonic adaptation, a vision is an expression of something lasting. A personal vision answers the question of how you would most like to spend your time in life. It focuses on actions, not results. It focuses on the journey, not the destination. As the old saying goes: *"The journey is the destination."*

INTRINSIC JOURNEY-BASED MOTIVATION:

1. A PERSONAL VISION DOESN'T FOCUS ON GOALS; IT FOCUSES ON THE JOURNEY. IT DESCRIBES THE TYPES OF ACTIVITIES YOU WOULD LIKE TO SPEND YOUR LIFE DOING.

On the way to living up to your vision, you can set *milestones*. They assure you that you are headed in the right direction and that you are truly moving forward. The difference between a goal and a milestone is that when people are motivated by goals, they work just to reach them. In contrast, a milestone is a helper, a landmark that provides you feedback about whether you are headed in the right direction.

For example, completing this book isn't a goal for me; it's a milestone. If everything goes well, I will know that I have done something real, something in line with my personal vision. I am not writing just to finish this book. I am writing so that I can help people better utilize their time and potential.

2. ALONG THE WAY YOU CAN SET MILESTONES. THESE DIFFER FROM GOALS IN THAT THEY GIVE YOU FEEDBACK ON WHETHER YOU ARE HEADED IN THE RIGHT DIRECTION.

The prime benefit of journey-based motivation is that it helps you be happy in the present more often. You don't need to reach a goal to be happy nor will you experience the negative emotions brought about by the stick of extrinsic motivation.

You will more often experience a state of *happiness now*—a sense of contentment with your present situation. If you do things that match your vision, you will get the feeling that everything is the way it should be. But this doesn't mean you are stuck in one place because your vision and its motivational effect drive you forward.

If your actions help you live up to your vision, it means you are doing exactly the things you want to do. Therefore, you are happier and your brain is flooded with more dopamine. Thanks to this, you are more creative, your brain and memory work better, and you are better able to learn. Thus, the skills required to perform actions that lead you to fulfilling your vision improve constantly. Every improvement increases the chances of seeing even further improvement. This positive *feedback loop* can help you achieve true *mastery*. This is why people who are motivated by their visions achieve things that not even the largest stick or the greatest goals can accomplish.

Studies on the most successful athletes, scientists, artists, and businesspeople show that they all have something in common.[38] The activities they do put them in a *state of flow*. You find your flow when you are up against a challenge and put your strengths and skills to work.[39] You become fully absorbed in what you are doing. Time stops for you. Unlike the **emotion of joy**, which is experienced only briefly after having achieved a goal, reaching a **state of flow** can release dopamine over the long term.

COMPARED TO THE EMOTION OF JOY, THE DOPAMINE
AS WELL AS THE HAPPINESS THAT ARE RELEASED DURING
THE STATE OF FLOW HAVE A LASTING EFFECT.

The mentioned studies on flow and hedonic adaptation indicate that long-term happiness can't be found in a material object, goal, or state. It's found in the journey, on the way to fulfilling your vision, in doing things that are meaningful for you.

4. FLOW ARISES IN SITUATIONS WHERE YOU FEEL CHALLENGED AND AT THE SAME TIME UTILIZE YOUR STRENGTHS. DOPAMINE IS RELEASED OVER THE LONG-TERM, MAKING YOU MORE CREATIVE, BETTER ABLE TO LEARN, AND HAPPIER. EVERY STEP TOWARDS YOUR VISION BRINGS YOU CLOSER TO MASTERY.

This approach is the exact opposite of the classic method of thinking which says: *"First results, then happiness."* The reality is paradoxically the opposite. First you must find **happiness** and thanks to it you will get **results**. As Albert Schweitzer, winner of the 1952 Nobel Peace Prize, proclaimed: *"Success is not the key to happiness. Happiness is the key to success. If you love what you are doing, you will be successful."*

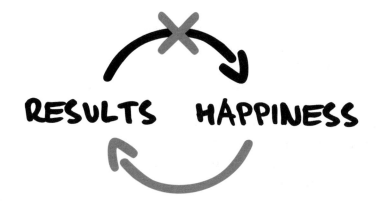

Why Meaning Is So Important

One evening I parked my car downtown and got out. At that very minute, a van pulled out a few feet away from me and hit another parked car. The van's driver, although he must have known he had hit a car, took off. For a moment, I just stood and stared in a daze.

Then, once I got myself together, I sat back behind the wheel of my car and took off after the van. I caught up with it three blocks away. I then passed it and stopped, blocking it. I climbed out and, using my cell phone, took a picture of the license plate and the part of the van that had been damaged. Then I returned to the car that had been hit. I wrote a note explaining what had happened and how to get in touch with me, and stuck it behind a wiper.

A few days later, the owner of that car came by to see me in person. He had read my note. A distinguished gentleman dressed in a blazer told me that everything had been worked out with the insurance company and that his car had been repaired. As I found out, he was the head surgeon at a nearby hospital—a man who spends his entire day, from morning until night, helping others. Nonetheless, he didn't take my relatively small efforts for granted and stopped by to thank me. At that moment, I experienced one of the strongest emotions possible: the emotion associated with feeling a sense of purpose, or what we call the *emotion of meaning*.

The things we do in life can be divided into two types of activities. The first comprise activities that you do just for yourself. These include, for example, behaviors that ensure that your basic needs are met along with your survival and development. We call them *ego-1.0 activities*. Then there are selfless acts. These are things that you do not do for yourself but for others, in earnest. We call them *ego-2.0 activities*. It is these acts that can produce a strong feeling—the **emotion of meaning**—resulting in a third type of happiness alongside those created by the **emotion of joy** and the **state of flow**.

5. WHEN YOU PERFORM SELFLESS ACTS, YOU ARE REWARDED WITH A STRONG FEELING: THE EMOTION OF MEANING.

Why is it good to include elements of selflessness and ego-2.0 activities in your personal vision? Why do people experience stronger positive emotions when they do things that have a "higher" purpose? Why did parts of our brain develop that support this type of behavior?

To illustrate this point, imagine an **individual unit** of something. It could be a single atom, molecule, or cell, or even an ant, elephant, or human being. Imagine that this individual entity has its own imaginary **potential** that it is trying to fulfill: an atom tries to bond with other atoms, a white blood cell tries to kill harmful bacteria, a person tries to live up to his or her personal vision.

1. AN INDIVIDUAL TRIES TO LIVE UP TO ITS POTENTIAL.

If there are many individuals near each other, sooner or later *self-organization* will occur. Individuals begin to spontaneously join together and create **communities** that help them live up to their potential more effectively. Self-organization helps create space for cooperation, or what is known as *group synergy*. The whole becomes greater than the sum of its parts ("1+1=3").

But that's not all. Self-organization takes place not only at the individual level but also at the group level. Groups sooner or later join together to create larger communities that help them function better. And so it continues on and on. Self-organization happens on the micro-scale

2. THANKS TO SELF-ORGANIZATION, INDIVIDUALS CREATE COMMUNITIES. RESULTING GROUP SYNERGY HELPS THEM TO LIVE UP TO THEIR POTENTIAL MORE EFFECTIVELY.

all the way up to the macro-scale. Atoms combine to form molecules, molecules combine to form cells, cells combine to create organisms, organisms combine to create communities, and so on.

Self-organization has been responsible for many turning points in the evolution of life on Earth. Take for example *Volvox globator*, a single-celled organism that at some point in its evolutionary history underwent a major transition in its lifestyle: individual organisms stopped living separately and began forming large colonies.[40] These spherical colonies are composed of hundreds of individual organisms that can move more effectively and work better as a group. They became a symbol of the transformation of single-celled organisms into multi-celled ones.

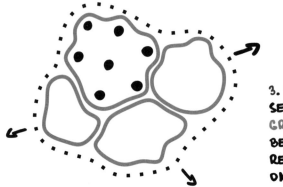

3. THANKS TO SELF-ORGANIZATION, GROUPS OF INDIVIDUALS BEGIN TO COMBINE, RESULTING IN SYNERGY ONCE AGAIN.

The same thing happened to solitary wasps, which more than 100 million years ago began cooperating to make nests, eventually giving rise to today's bees, ants, and other species of social insects that colonized the whole world.[41] Moreover, every single cell in our bodies is evidence of self-organization. It contains organelles known as mitochondria which have completely different DNA than the cell's nucleus. This is due to the fact that, at an earlier point in history, mitochondria were most likely free-living organisms.[42]

When our ancestors first began meeting around a communal fire, it was an important dividing point in the evolution of society. The communities that developed were better at dividing labor, exchanging goods, and protecting themselves, and they were capable of effectively spreading thoughts, technology, and culture.[43] What supported this type of development? Why have we humans evolved to become team players?

Darwin's theory of evolution is based on the survival of the fittest. Fitter individuals are more capable of breeding and passing on their traits to their offspring. Those incapable of competing perish, and their genetic information is lost. But Darwin also described what is known as *group selection*. Just as individuals compete amongst each other for survival, so do groups of individuals.[44]

Imagine two tribes of prehistoric mammoth hunters. One of these tribes works together: they split up tasks, they protect each other, and, once they have completed a successful hunt, they share their prey. The other tribe is a group of selfish individualists. Everyone expects that it will be someone else who will stick their neck out in the mammoth hunt; they don't work together, and if, despite this, the group succeeds, they end up fighting over who will get the biggest piece of meat. Which group has the greatest chance of surviving?

The scientific discipline called *game theory*, for which the Nobel Prize for Economics was awarded in 1994, proves from a mathematical point of view that it is better for individuals to work together and to behave selflessly.[45] In the long term this type of behavior is more advantageous than behaving purely selfishly. The more cooperating individuals there are in a group, the greater its chances of survival are.

Prehistoric humans were probably not familiar with game theory and therefore could not have possibly based their actions on it, but nonetheless they began to work together. Why?

GROUP SELECTION:

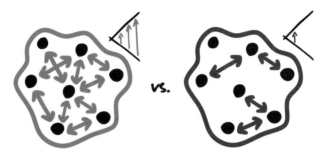

THANKS TO GROUP SELECTION, GROUPS MADE UP OF MORE COOPERATING INDIVIDUALS HAVE A GREATER CHANCE OF SURVIVING.

Emotions have gradually developed for the purpose of supporting rational behavior. For example, the feeling of thirst evolved to remind us to drink so that we do not die from a lack of water. Similarly, this is most likely how the **emotion of meaning** evolved—our reward for cooperating and behaving selflessly. Experiencing this emotion supports self-organization and **ego-2.0 activities**.

Since the dawn of time, thinkers have been dealing with the question of how to define **good** and **evil**. From the viewpoint of self-organization, acts driven by ego-2.0 can be classified as *elementary good*. Individuals can do things that help not only themselves but also other individuals and the communities of which they are a part. This ability to cooperate selflessly leads to the development of both individuals and entire groups.

The opposite of elementary good could be *elementary evil*—selfish behavior through which an individual harms the other individuals and the communities to which it belongs for its own benefit. Take for example the behavior of cancer cells which damage the body of their host with their unrestricted growth.

The Power of a Group Vision

"We need to group together. If you want to change the world, you have to group together, you have to be collaborative." This idea put forth by Swiss philosopher Alain de Botton contains the key to *group motivation.*

If the members of a group all have similar values and **personal visions**, it becomes much easier to found movements, organizations, or other associations that can really move things forward. If people come together to create a **group vision**, the result is very strong group motivation. If your personal vision matches the vision of the community you are a part of, you will experience the shared emotion of meaning. It is this emotion that has been one of the most important driving forces in human history—it has toppled dictators, launched revolutions, and initiated other changes that have transformed the entire world.

There are many examples of how this shared emotion of meaning can be experienced by people all across the globe. Practically every single world religion works on this principle, sports fans experience it when rooting for their teams, and it can be documented in the experiences of combat veterans.[46]

Group motivation based on shared values and vision was also the key to forming employee dedication in most of the inspiring companies I visited. The shared vision at Novo Nordisk which gives their employees a deeper meaning is just one example.

Simon Sinek described the power of group vision when he said: *"If you hire people just because they can do a job, they'll work for your money. But if you hire people who believe what you believe, they'll work for you with blood and sweat and tears."*

So What Kind of Motivation Is the Most Beneficial?

If you want to fight procrastination and be happy at the same time, you need to choose the right type of motivation. As research findings indicate, this shouldn't be extrinsic stick-based motivation nor should it be intrinsic goal-based motivation. The most effective type of motivation involves getting rid of sticks and goals and creating a personal vision that triggers intrinsic journey-based motivation.

A vision, however, would not be such a strong motivator if it just involved performing selfish ego-1.0 acts. Only activities that result in elementary good—selfless ego-2.0 acts—can release the emotion of meaning, one of the strongest emotions that you can experience.

This type of motivation will constantly drive you forward, pulling you ahead like a strong magnet. At the same time you will experience

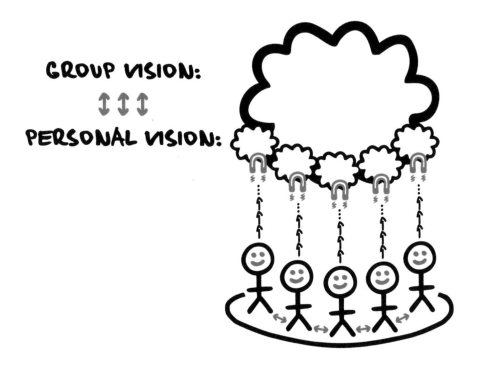

GROUP VISION:

PERSONAL VISION:

IF YOU TEAM UP WITH PEOPLE THAT HAVE SIMILAR VALUES AND PERSONAL VISIONS, A VERY STRONG GROUP MOTIVATION IS CREATED.

a state of flow and the emotion of meaning, which will bring you many positive feelings, putting you in a lasting state of happiness now.

If you surround yourself with people who have a similar vision, you can collaborate with them and create a community. Thus, group motivation is born, magnifying the effects of your personal vision.

How can you create a Personal vision? If you have no idea, don't worry. The following section will help you.

TOOL: A Personal Vision

"Your time is limited, so don't waste it living someone else's life. Don't be trapped by dogma—which is living with the results of other people's thinking." Steve Jobs shared this idea with the graduating class of Stanford University in 2005.

Choosing the right type of motivation is crucial for your personal development and reducing procrastination. Therefore, the first practical tool we will share with you in this book is how to create a **Personal vision**, setting the stage for **journey-based motivation**. This type of motivation will make your vision have a lasting effect and will lead not only to results but also to you being more happy more often. And because we are talking about your life and the responsibility you have for it, you need to create your own Personal vision. Never forgot the word "personal" in the tool's name.

Once a client asked me to create his vision for him. He was willing to pay for the service; he claimed he just didn't have the time to do it himself. I explained to him that it wouldn't work. In order for a vision to spark the engine of intrinsic motivation, it must be an expression of *autonomy*; it must be your own vision—the fruit of your labors—containing your thoughts and values.

How can you create your vision? Before you begin, we recommend getting ready by taking a few simple steps. We have developed the following support tools to help you discover useful information about yourself that will later help you form the final version of your Personal vision.

- **A Personal SWOT Analysis** will uncover your strengths and weaknesses. It will also help you identify threats that may stop you from moving forward as well as find new opportunities.
- **A List of Personal Achievements** will help you write down the things you have accomplished in life and which make you proud of yourself.
- **An Analysis of Motivating Activities** will help you map out the things you want to do in life. There are four types of activities that can generate powerful motivation.
- **A Beta Version of Your Personal Vision** will help you lay the foundations for your final vision. The early phases of creating a vision are the most important, but at the same time people often procrastinate doing them. This method will simplify the process and allow you to really get started.

Find yourself one free afternoon and get to work in peace and quiet. You will find detailed instructions about how to do this on the following pages. Working on your Personal vision requires time. Don't rush yourself. As you work, you'll find that you are gradually progressing towards producing a **final version of your vision**.

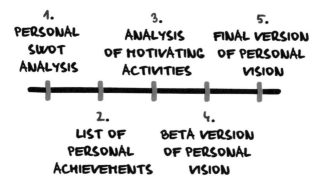

1. PERSONAL SWOT ANALYSIS
2. LIST OF PERSONAL ACHIEVEMENTS
3. ANALYSIS OF MOTIVATING ACTIVITIES
4. BETA VERSION OF PERSONAL VISION
5. FINAL VERSION OF PERSONAL VISION

Personal SWOT Analysis

Are you creative but sometimes disorganized? Or are you precise and analytical but occasionally incapable of improvising? I often ask people what their strengths and weaknesses are and what kind of activities they enjoy doing and what kind they don't. It is interesting to note that even though these are relatively important questions, people often don't have the answers to them. A **personal SWOT* analysis** will help you find these answers.

The first thing you need to do is fill out the top row of the SWOT analysis chart. Ask yourself the question: "What are my **strengths** and **weaknesses**?" Try to come up with at least five strengths and five weaknesses. What's the point of all this?

---

*   **S** = Strengths, **W** = Weaknesses, **O** = Opportunities, **T** = Threats.

You should put your strengths to use for the activities you will perform most often to fulfill your vision. When you have the skills and feel a sense of meaning, flow is born. In contrast, weaknesses are flow's enemies, so be careful of yours when creating your vision. If you lack the skills to perform a certain activity, but nonetheless that activity is important for fulfilling your vision, you will only end up feeling anxious and frustrated.

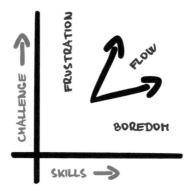

At one time our company had an accountant who managed to lose three years' worth of financial records. I remember what it was like walking into his office filled with never-ending stacks of random papers. I think that precision, one of the strengths that every accountant should have, was a characteristic that he completely lacked. After about five months, when he stopped communicating with us for good, he found the records we needed and returned them to us. I don't think he was a bad person, nor do I think his behavior was intentional. What I think is that he misjudged his abilities. This experience has reassured me in my thinking that people should take into account their strengths and weaknesses when they choose a career or what type of education to pursue. This is particularly true for creating a Personal vision.

How much time should you spend working on your weaknesses? In my experience, although it is definitely useful to work on your weaknesses, I think you should spend more time developing your strengths. I have discovered that my ideal ratio is 80:20. This means I spend an entire 80 percent of my time developing my strengths whereas I dedicate just 20 percent to struggling with my weaknesses.

A Personal vision shouldn't just challenge you and point you in the right direction. It is also important to make sure that the main activities you do leading you to the fulfillment of your Personal vision consist of your strengths.

In writing these words, I don't feel the same flow I would as if I was personally saying the same words to you at one of my seminars. Even though I see the same meaning in both of these activities—writing and speaking—speaking has always come naturally to me, whereas I never considered writing to be one of my strengths. That is why my own Personal vision relies more on my training skills than my literary abilities.

But let's get back to the SWOT analysis. The next step is to fill in **opportunities** and **threats**. By thinking about the opportunities you have in life, you can discover the possibilities the world can offer you. When creating your vision, it is important to pick out only key opportunities and slam the door in the face of others. One of the most important characteristics of a Personal vision is that it can help you fight decision paralysis as well as select the most important opportunities that the wide-open scissors of potential offer.

If you leave multiple back doors open, you will end up being less satisfied with the path you have chosen.[47] By intentionally closing the scissors of potential, it makes it easier for you to live up to your potential.

For example, imagine someone who thinks daily about whether to move to New Zealand, to change jobs, or to find a new partner. This will repetitively drain his energy. However, if you are able to make a long-term or even permanent decision instead of spending your days hesitating, you will be able to focus on the things that you have decided are important.

Analyzing threats is important as a preventative measure. You should always think about the obstacles life might throw at you. Often people discover that no significant threats face them. This discovery helps relax worries and eliminate fear of the future and gives a greater feeling of assurance.

If you aren't sure about any part of your SWOT analysis, don't worry. You can always come back to it at anytime in the future. The main idea behind conducting this analysis is to get you thinking about these four aspects of your life in order to help you create a final version of your Personal vision.

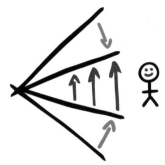

A PERSONAL VISION WILL HELP YOU PICK OUT THE MOST IMPORTANT OPPORTUNITIES. BY LIMITING THE SCOPE OF YOUR POTENTIAL, YOU WILL BE ABLE TO LIVE UP TO IT MORE EASILY.

A List of Personal Achievements

Take some blank white paper and make a list of your most important accomplishments in life. Write down things that make you proud of yourself. Keep writing until you have at least ten items. This too will take some time. So, make yourself free for an hour, find a pleasant spot, take a pen and paper, and write down whatever comes to mind.

A certain client of mine confided in me that this was the first time he had ever thought about his achievements. He told me that as he wrote them down, he was reminded of things he had long ago forgotten. He even brought a 24-item list to our next meeting. When he read it, I could sense his enthusiasm and improved self-confidence; both of these feelings are critical for working on the final version of your vision. A list of personal achievements will encourage positive emotions every time you look at it.

A LIST OF PERSONAL ACHIEVEMENTS:

An Analysis of Motivational Activities

What kind of things would you like to do for your development? Do you want to learn something new? Exercise? Eat more healthily? What kind of activities would you like to perform in order to leave your mark on the world? What do you want to do to build relationships with other people? How kind of ego-2.0 activities can you do?

An analysis of motivational activities can help discover things that, when included in your Personal vision, can create a strong intrinsic motivation. For clarity's sake, these activities can be divided into four groups:

- **Development activities** – These include education, skill development, sports, living a healthy lifestyle, and developing effective rest techniques.
- **Legacy-creating activities** – Your legacy is what you leave behind in this world. These activities can result in a physical legacy (i.e. planting trees, building a house), or they can be intangible (i.e. passing on ideas and values to others). Bringing up a child is a good example of the latter.
- **Relationship-building activities** – Humans are social creatures, and therefore making connections with other people is very important. These are activities that see you involved with your family and friends or creating new business contacts.

- **Ego 2.0-driven activities** – These are selfless acts that you don't do for yourself but for those around you. They can be things that help other people, or activities that improve how society works. Overall, they are acts that have a deeper meaning.

A well-balanced Personal vision should include activities that complement each other and that cover all four of the above-described areas. For example, for me writing this book is an activity that does indeed cover all of these areas. It develops my literary skills and at the same creates a legacy of my thoughts. This book has made meeting new people possible, and I believe that it will help its readers improve their lives.

Filling in the following chart will move you towards crafting the final Personal vision. For each type of activity, try to come up with at least three ideas of things that you would like to do in life.

The Beta Version of Your Personal Vision

That last support method to help you create the final version of your Personal vision is its draft: a **beta version**. In my experience, people most frequently put things off and procrastinate when it comes to starting work on their vision. Therefore, a beta version makes the first step of work on your final vision all too easy. It will also increase the odds of you continuing to work on it and eventually finishing it.

If you can answer the following questions, you already have a beta version of your Personal vision.

1. DEVELOPMENT:

2. LEGACY:

3. RELATIONSHIPS:

4. EGO-2.0:

THE BETA VERSION OF YOUR VISION:

1. WHAT ARE YOUR FAVORITE QUOTES? WHAT THOUGHTS RESONATE STRONGLY WITH YOU?

2. WHAT ARE YOUR THREE MOST IMPORTANT VALUES IN LIFE?

3. HOW WOULD YOU LIKE TO SPEND YOUR TIME? WHAT KIND OF THINGS WOULD YOU IDEALLY LIKE TO DO?

4. HOW CAN YOU CONTRIBUTE TO SOCIETY? WHAT KIND OF EGO-2.0 ACTS CAN YOU PERFORM?

The Final Version of Your Vision

What should the final vision ideally look like? As autonomy is a key element in creating your vision, the final form is mainly up to you. Your vision statement may be several paragraphs long, or it may just contain a few lines of text. It is mainly supposed to evoke the associations, thoughts, and emotions you want it to. Nonetheless, you should follow a few basic recommendations in order to help you increase the chance of your vision having long-lasting effects.

- **Tangible form** – It really pays off to write your vision down on a piece of paper. This way you can carry it with you, hang it up somewhere, look at it, and read it regularly. Our brains have an amazing tendency to forget even the most important of things, including our Personal vision. You might go to bed with your vision crystal clear in your head, but the next morning you can wake up and find it gone. Having a written version will serve as a constant reminder so that, for example, when you do wake up in the morning you will recall the main ideas. Writing your vision down will also allow you to update and modify it and will lead to a more perfect version.

- **Emotional response** – To increase emotional response, you can add some of your favorite quotations or ideas that resonate strongly with you. A picture or photograph can have a similar effect in that it can evoke the right associations. Your vision, just like this book, can contain diagrams, drawings, or any other graphic elements. It can become your own private work of art.

- **Focus on action, not goals** – As I explained earlier, people often fall into the trap of hedonic adaptation. If you don't want to become addicted to goals, your vision should focus on your journey, not goals. For example, your vision might include a statement that starts: "My purpose in life is to do..." By focusing on the journey you will work your way towards achieving a state of flow, making you happier now.
- **Incorporate ego-2.0 activities** – If your vision is too selfish in aim, it won't help you experience the emotion of meaning. Therefore your vision should include both ego-1.0 activities as well as ego-2.0 ones. Inventor Nikola Tesla described his vision: *"Everything I did, I did for mankind, for a world where there would be no humiliation of the poor by the violence of the rich, where products of intellect, science and art will serve society for the betterment and beautification of life."*
- **Balance and connectedness** – Your Personal vision should be balanced and should cover your work life as well as your personal and family life. Seeing as you cannot devote one hundred percent of your time and energy to everything, you need to determine priorities and the amount of time you wish to spend on each activity. Your Personal vision should also be coherent. This means that all of its parts should work together in harmony. There should be no fundamental conflicts, meaning that living up to one part of your vision will negate your ability to fulfill another aspect.
- **Use anchors** – Anchors are physical objects that remind you of your vision. I personally have a ring that I made myself when I was young.

It has a unique shape, which I use as my vision's symbol. Whenever I want to remind myself of my vision and I don't have my paper version on hand, I twist my ring a few times. Rituals help your brain connect objects—the anchors you have chosen—with the ideas your vision contains. Jewelry or a watch you inherited, a picture, your computer background, a certain symbol, a favorite song, or even certain alarm clock tones can all serve as anchors.

Creating and bettering your vision can be a life-long process. Even though your vision may seem perfect now, in the future new situations may arise requiring you to improve it.

Creating a Personal vision is the first and most important step in effectively fighting procrastination. Unfortunately, it is also a step that people often put off. **Don't procrastinate when it comes to fighting procrastination.**

Ideally, you should plan to spend one entire free afternoon going through these outlined steps and creating a first version of your Personal vision. Just to be sure, schedule this activity into your calendar right now. We have created some printable worksheets to help you. You can find them at **www.procrastination.com/personal-vision**.

IDEAS FOR PUTTING YOUR VISION INTO ACTION:

1. WHAT CAN YOU DO TO USE YOUR VISION EVERY DAY?

2. WHAT STEPS CAN YOU TAKE TO REGULARLY IMPROVE YOUR VISION?

3. WHAT CAN YOU DO TO NEVER FORGET YOUR VISION?

4. WHAT SPECIFIC ACTIONS WILL YOU TAKE TO UTILIZE YOUR PERSONAL VISION TO THE FULLEST?

Chapter Recap: Motivation

The more motivated you are, the less you will procrastinate. Not all types of motivation have the same effect on happiness.

The stick of **extrinsic motivation** creates pressure on people to do things they ordinarily would have no desire to do. The result is unhappiness, which causes the brain to release less dopamine. This leads to worsened brain function, lower creativity, and poor memory and learning capacity.

When you are motivated by **intrinsic goal-based motivation**, due to hedonic adaptation, achieving goals only produces a temporary state of happiness: the **emotion of joy**. This emotion can cause addiction.

Intrinsic journey-based motivation, instead of focusing on goals, concentrates on the activities that you would like to do. Thanks to this, hedonic adaptation is overcome, allowing you to experience **happiness now** more often.

When you do the things you want to do and which incorporate your strengths, you will achieve a **state of flow**. Your brain will constantly release more dopamine, resulting in higher levels of creativity and more effective learning abilities, which will help you reach **mastery**.

Incorporating selfless **ego-2.0 activities** in your vision will result in the **emotion of meaning**. Meaning improves the effectiveness of intrinsic motivation and helps you experience living your life to the fullest more intensely.

A **Personal vision** is the main tool that will kick-start intrinsic journey-based motivation. It will help you determine priorities, reduce decision paralysis, and lead you to doing things that are truly meaningful.

If you team up with people who share similar values and personal visions, a powerful **group vision** may arise. This results in a very intense form of group motivation.

Several support tools can be used to create a Personal vision: **a personal SWOT analysis**, **a list of personal achievements**, **an analysis of motivational activities**, and the creation of **a beta version of your Personal vision**.

As **autonomy** is so important, the final version of your vision is dependent mainly on you, its owner. Nonetheless, there are some common steps you can take to increase its effectiveness: tangible form, emotional response, focusing on actions not goals, incorporating ego-2.0 activities, ensuring balance and connectedness, and using anchors as reminders.

To monitor your long-term progress, rate your current motivation and how you are using your Personal vision tool on a scale from 1 to 10.

1..10

☐ **MOTIVATION**

☐ **TOOL: PERSONAL VISION**

I don't expect that every reader will be able to create a perfect vision after having read this book just once. Making just minute improvements to the areas of your life covered in this chapter may result in large positive changes in the future. If you keep coming back to the main ideas contained in this chapter, I believe that at some point you will come up with a vision that will receive a top rating. I wish you lots of strength in looking for, and finding, your Personal vision.

DISCIPLINE

HOW TO GIVE YOURSELF ORDERS AND FOLLOW THEM

Back in college, I shared a dorm room with a future architect. He was an intelligent and talented individual and a good friend, but he was also one of the biggest procrastinators I have ever met. He had mastered the art of hitting the snooze button. Sometimes his alarm clock would go off at ten-minute intervals all the way until lunch. His specialty was doing almost everything at the last minute. He made it a rule to work on school projects only the night before they were due, and he was usually busy right until the morning. Sometimes he completed them, but often enough he didn't manage to get them done. I used to be a bit similar to him.

However, you don't have to put up with stress, poor sleeping habits, guilt, and problems snowballing out of control forever. You can break your procrastination habit if you know how.

Can you recall a time when you knew exactly what you were supposed to do but nonetheless you didn't do it? Do you sometimes find that you are unable to listen to yourself? One of the main reasons people procrastinate is a lack of discipline: the skill of convincing your body to perform a desired action.

Discipline is the second most important element of personal development, right after motivation. At its core is *self-regulation*—the ability to overcome the negative emotions that cause us to avoid completing tasks. Another important aspect is the ability to manage *decision paralysis*. The final factor involved in discipline is a concept we call *heroism*, which is based on the art of stepping outside of your comfort zone.

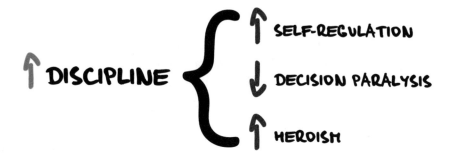

↑ DISCIPLINE {
↑ SELF-REGULATION
↓ DECISION PARALYSIS
↑ HEROISM

This chapter is based upon practical tools that can help you make lasting improvements to your discipline. Greater discipline will make you more productive and effective, and thus, you will be able to do more meaningful things. By living up to your personal vision more effectively, you will feel happier.

When Reason Says Yes, but Your Emotions Say No

My dad always used to say, *"Petr, you need to learn how to give yourself orders."* I would always answer: *"What do you mean, Dad? I tell myself what to do, I just don't listen."* The most extensive meta-analysis of studies on procrastination ever conducted indicates that failure of the ability to listen to ourselves is most likely the main reason why we put things off.[48] The scientific name of this ability is **self-regulation**.

SELF-REGULATION = THE SKILL OF GIVING YOURSELF ORDERS AND FOLLOWING THEM.

What's it like when you want to jump into a cold pool, but your body says no? How do you feel when you want to start up a conversation with a stranger but instead you just stand there silently? How many times have you told yourself that you are going to start working on something but spend the next few hours doing something else altogether? How many times in your life have you tried telling yourself what to do and haven't obeyed?

The reason we are incapable of obeying ourselves is buried in the history of how the human brain has evolved. Over the course of millions of years, our brains have not only grown in size, but they have also developed new parts.[49]

The oldest part of the human brain is the brainstem, also known as the *reptilian brain*. It is responsible for basic reflexes and instincts. Later, the *limbic system*, the part of the brain responsible for emotions, evolved in our mammalian ancestors. Much later, the youngest part of our brain, the *neocortex*, appeared. It is responsible for rational and logical thinking, planning, and language.[50]

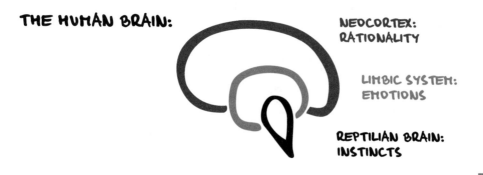

THE HUMAN BRAIN:

NEOCORTEX:
RATIONALITY

LIMBIC SYSTEM:
EMOTIONS

REPTILIAN BRAIN:
INSTINCTS

Since the brain developed gradually over time, the connections from the older limbic system to the newer neocortex are more numerous and much stronger than the connections going the other way.[51] The end result is that our behavior is much more greatly influenced by emotion than reason. Therefore, it is the structure of the brain that makes people so bad at obeying themselves. It is the rational neocortex that gives orders, but it is the stronger emotional limbic system that doesn't listen.

Self-regulation is the ability to consciously control your emotions. The more developed this ability is, the more often you will do what you tell yourself to do and the better you will resist temptation. Thanks to this, you will procrastinate less.

The skill of self-regulation is not about shutting off your emotions. Emotions by themselves are not bad. The opposite is true. They make decision-making easier, respond faster than reason, and thus contribute to survival. By building up your self-regulation skills, you can avoid the

THE WAY IN WHICH THE BRAIN EVOLVED RESULTED IN MORE NUMEROUS CONNECTIONS FROM THE EMOTIONAL BRAIN TO THE RATIONAL BRAIN.

trap of falling slave to your emotions in situations where they are not beneficial.

Some emotions evolved in completely different environments than the one we live in today. For example, the fear of approaching strangers most likely developed at a time in history when we were still living in small groups in caves, back when strangers could have posed serious threats. Today, however, the world is changing faster than our emotions can adapt. Thus, they often react inappropriately and cease to be our helpers. They become a barrier that you need to learn how to overcome. This is why self-regulation is so important.

How can you gain control of the emotions that are slowing you down? How can you overcome the negative emotions that paralyze you, the ones that make you procrastinate? How can you improve your ability to self-regulate? The solution can be elegantly demonstrated using the old Buddhist *metaphor of the elephant and rider*. It is so simple and illustrative that it is used in contemporary psychology.[52]

EVERYONE'S PERSONALITY CAN BE DIVIDED INTO TWO INDEPENDENT CREATURES: AN ELEPHANT AND A RIDER.

The Emotional Elephant and the Rational Rider

Figuratively speaking, every one of us has two independent creatures inside: a wild **elephant** and a **rider** that controls it. The elephant symbolizes our **emotions**, whereas the rider is our **rational side**. The difference in size between the elephant and the rider captures the imbalance of connections between the emotional limbic system and the rational neocortex.

Self-regulation is the ability of the rider to control the elephant. The more competent and stronger the rider is, the better he will be able to keep the elephant in line and guide him in the right direction. But if the rider is weak or tired, he loses his ability to control the elephant.

SELF-REGULATION

THE RIDER REPRESENTS RATIONALITY AND THE ELEPHANT EMOTIONS. SELF-REGULATION IS THE RIDER'S ABILITY TO CONTROL THE ELEPHANT.

Just as the rider must learn to control his elephant in order to guide him in the right direction, we must learn to consciously control our emotions so that we can take the right steps towards fulfilling our personal visions. It is not enough if your rider wants to follow your vision. Your elephant needs to as well. When there is harmony between the rider and elephant, you are in a state of flow. Your elephant enjoys the activity and your rider knows that what you are doing is in line with your vision.

How can you learn to control the elephant? How can you tame him? What is the ability to self-regulate based on?

HARMONY BETWEEN THE RIDER AND THE ELEPHANT IS CRITICAL FOR FULFILLING YOUR PERSONAL VISION.

Cognitive Resources: The Key to Self-Regulation

Studies show that your ability to self-regulate is limited and dependent on what are called *cognitive resources*.[53] In the case of the elephant and the rider, the available cognitive resources are represented by the rider's current energy level. Imagine it as if it were a glass of water. Every time you persuade yourself to act, your cognitive resources are drained— water is poured out of the glass.

COGNITIVE RESOURCES REPRESENT THE RIDER'S ENERGY. EVERY ACT OF SELF-REGULATION LOWERS THEIR LEVEL.

Once you have used up all of your cognitive resources, you lose your ability to self-regulate, and your emotions take over.[54] The rider loses energy and no longer has the strength to control the elephant. The elephant begins to do whatever it wants. It begins to watch TV on you, to compulsively go on Facebook, to drink, to smoke, to cheat, to overeat, to watch porn, or to go on mindless shopping sprees. The elephant is beginning to procrastinate on you.

ONCE COGNITIVE RESOURCES HAVE BEEN EXHAUSTED, THE RIDER IS NO LONGER CAPABLE OF CONTROLLING THE ELEPHANT. IT BEGINS DOING WHATEVER IT WANTS.

The good news is that you can **replenish** your cognitive resources throughout the day, and it is even possible to **increase** their total capacity. This means that not only can you refill your imaginary glass, you can also make it bigger.

Replenishing Your Cognitive Resources

If you want to be able to self-regulate all day long, you need to regularly replenish your cognitive resources. You need to pour water into the glass.

YOUR COGNITIVE RESOURCES CAN BE REPLENISHED THROUGHOUT THE DAY. THIS WILL HELP YOU SELF-REGULATE BETTER.

You should refill **regularly as a preventative measure**; it is not a good idea to put it off. If you procrastinate when it comes time to rest, you risk fully draining your cognitive resources to the point that you will no longer have the energy to replenish it.

Studies indicate that cognitive resources are to a large extent dependent on nutrients, especially glucose and simple sugars.[55] Therefore, to replenish your ability to self-regulate, it is good to drink a little fresh juice or eat some fruit. Another way to regenerate is to spend some time doing non-demanding manual or physical activities that allow your rider to relax.[56] A five-minute walk can almost recharge your rider to full power.[57]

Thus, several times a day you should shut your phone off, drink a glass of juice, and take a walk around the block by yourself. The time you spend doing this will help replenish your cognitive resources, and you will be able to do more activities that require self-regulation. The regular preventative renewal of your cognitive resource can multiply your productivity.

Many of my clients confide in me that they work long into the night and that they are literally squeezed dry. I used to be the same way. I have since learned how to plan regular rest into my day and, most importantly, how to follow these plans. If I remember to replenish my cognitive resources, sometimes I end the work day with more energy than I had in the morning.

Increasing Your Cognitive Resources

When someone is said to have a strong will, this usually means that the capacity of his or her cognitive resources is very large. The bigger your glass is, the longer you can self-regulate.

In contrast, procrastinators have a very low capacity for self-regulation, and therefore their riders become rapidly exhausted. Current research indicates that willpower can be compared to a muscle.[58] It is possible to strengthen it through training; this will help improve the performance of your rider.

It is possible not only to strengthen your **willpower muscle**, but also to wear it down. This is why making too many or too far-reaching New

Year's resolutions is not such a great idea. They will have the same effect on your willpower as doing a seriously intense workout at the gym once a year has on your muscles. Short, temporary bursts of activity won't help your willpower, just like they won't help your muscles. In fact, such activity may worsen the situation. Therefore, you need to approach working on your cognitive resources very cautiously.

Expanding your cognitive resources is the base of improving self-regulation and thus the base for effectively fighting procrastination over the long term. The key to strengthening your willpower muscle is in having the right approach to **building habits**.

 YOU CAN INCREASE YOUR COGNITIVE RESOURCES THROUGH TRAINING. IT WILL THEN LAST LONGER BEFORE BECOMING FULLY EXHAUSTED.

Building Habits: How to Train Your Elephant

Recently, one of my colleagues trained for, and then ran, a 70 mile-long mountain ultramarathon. Just a few years ago, he didn't run at all, and in fact, running was a sport he didn't like. I now consider this formerly irresponsible procrastinator to have one of the strongest willpower muscles of anyone I know. By gradually building habits, he was able to get his elephant into gear.

Many things you need to do in life are unpleasant at first. This results in **emotional aversion**, which paralyzes you and causes you to put things off. Even if reasoning tells you that a certain task must be done, negative emotions will discourage you from doing it. Your elephant will see it as an obstacle and will become afraid. The greater your aversion (the greater and more complicated the task is), the greater obstacle it presents to the elephant.

EMOTIONAL AVERSION **IS AN OBSTACLE THAT LEADS TO PARALYSIS AND THE INABILITY TO PERFORM** RATIONALLY PLANNED ACTIONS.

Many important things in life lie on the other side of these emotional barriers, and therefore you need to learn how to overcome them. How can you handle aversion? How can you even learn to like unpleasant activities? How can you learn to gradually catch your flow while doing them?

To overcome paralysis, you need to start by **setting the bar as low as possible** so that your elephant is not afraid. Then, teach your elephant how to go over this low obstacle. You can accomplish this through regular repetition. Usually actions need to be repeated **twenty or thirty times**.[59] It will then become an automatic activity for the elephant; you

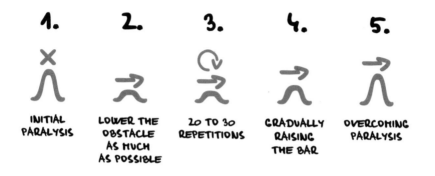

1. INITIAL PARALYSIS

2. LOWER THE OBSTACLE AS MUCH AS POSSIBLE

3. 20 TO 30 REPETITIONS

4. GRADUALLY RAISING THE BAR

5. OVERCOMING PARALYSIS

will have learned a new habit. You will feel no aversion to doing it; it will be like brushing your teeth.

Once you begin managing your new habit, you can **slowly raise the bar**. This way you can learn to overcome the obstacles that initially caused aversion and led to paralysis.

This is how I started writing this book. I told myself that every day I would write only two paragraphs. For me, and particularly for my elephant, this amount of writing was acceptable. If from the very get-go I told myself that I would write several pages or even an entire chapter, it is quite likely that you wouldn't be reading this book right now.

Creating habits isn't about quantity; it's about small steps and regular repetition. By taking small steps, you can make big changes. Long ago, Japanese samurais used a method of gradual, constant learning to overcome even the most unpleasant of things. They called it *kaizen*.[60]

HOW TO LEARN HABITS:

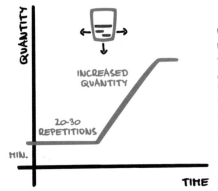

WHEN LEARNING NEW HABITS, IT IS IMPORTANT TO SET THE BAR AS LOW AS POSSIBLE AT THE BEGINNING. ONCE YOU MANAGE A NEW HABIT, YOU CAN START INCREASING THE QUANTITY. THIS WILL HELP TRAIN YOUR WILLPOWER MUSCLE.

By making gradual increases once you learn a new habit, you can strengthen your willpower muscle. As you slowly raise the bar, your willpower will gain strength. The more powerful it is, the easier it will be for you to overcome more and more obstacles.

If you want to start running, it wouldn't be the best idea to go out and run two miles. Setting the bar too high will most likely frighten your elephant; you might go running once or twice but that would most likely be where your running career ends.

If you want to make a habit out of running, you have to start out with as little to overcome as possible. Go outside and run a few hundred feet every day. Or just put on some athletic clothes, go outside, then come back in. There is always a step that the elephant will be comfortable taking. If you can repeat this small step a few times, your elephant will grow accustomed to it and you will be able to start lengthening your runs. You can use this method to teach yourself how to run almost any distance. Since you will begin catching flow while running, you'll start enjoying it.

Learning how to wake up early, eat healthily, exercise regularly, or eliminate bad habits can all be achieved by taking small steps, too. Gradual changes are more pleasant than sudden, radical shifts. They are more enduring, and therefore the odds of success are much higher.

Because you only have one willpower muscle for everything, if you train it to perform one activity, you can use its strength to do other things as well. My colleague, who trained his willpower by running, now uses it at work every day.

How to Not Disrupt Habits and How to Maintain Them

Habits can be disrupted fairly easily by vacations, sickness, or just plain forgetfulness. When this happens though, you need to know how to get back to your habit as soon as possible. After a pause, many people have a tendency to make a critical mistake that scares the elephant and causes them to fall out of their habit: they will want to start where they left off before the pause. For example, after being sick you will want to go out and run the two miles you had worked yourself up to. However, immediately returning to the same level of intensity is a jarring shock that can elicit aversion in your elephant.

So once you break a habit, you should return to **setting the bar as low as possible**. After doing a few repetitions, you will be ready to begin increasing your performance once again. When it comes to building habits, changes always need to be made slowly.

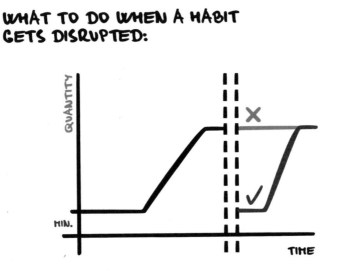

WHAT TO DO WHEN A HABIT GETS DISRUPTED:

IF ONE OF YOUR HABITS IS DISRUPTED, IT IS NOT A GOOD IDEA TO START WHERE YOU LEFT OFF; THIS COULD LEAD TO PARALYSIS. IT IS A SAFE BET TO GO BACK TO YOUR MINIMUM TARGET AND REPEAT IT A FEW TIMES. ONLY THEN SHOULD YOU BEGIN INCREASING YOUR PERFORMANCE AGAIN.

How to Break Bad Habits and Leave Them for Good

You can use the same methods for learning **new habits** to break **bad habits**. By gradually limiting bad habits *kaizen-style*, you can eventually get rid of them.

One of my clients used to smoke a pack and a half of cigarettes a day. As he had tried many times to quit and always failed, he had lost faith in himself; he thought he was incapable of ending his bad habit. Thus, together we decided he should try the *kaizen* method.

He set a limit for the first month: one pack a day. This didn't bring out much aversion in his elephant. Once he got past the twenty-day mark, he began slowly reducing his daily consumption. During the second month, he went from twenty, to fifteen, to ten a day. In the third month, he managed to go from ten, to five, all the way to zero. Today, he can proudly say he hasn't smoked a cigarette in a year and a half.

Using the same method, we have been able to turn alcoholics into non-drinkers and people who never exercised into athletes. One of my clients learned to stop biting his nails and yet another learned to enjoy ironing laundry. All of these changes were made gradually, which is why they have been lasting.

You can improve your struggle against bad habits by purposefully **eliciting aversion**. Put obstacles in the elephant's way. For example, you can purposefully "hide" a Facebook icon in a subfolder and this will lower the probability of you clicking on it so often.

BREAKING BAD HABITS:

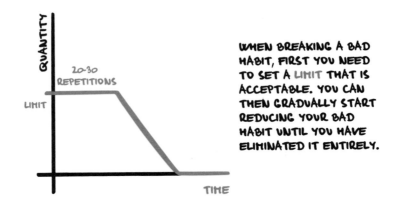

WHEN BREAKING A BAD HABIT, FIRST YOU NEED TO SET A LIMIT THAT IS ACCEPTABLE. YOU CAN THEN GRADUALLY START REDUCING YOUR BAD HABIT UNTIL YOU HAVE ELIMINATED IT ENTIRELY.

A friend of mine used this principle to stop smoking. He promised himself that for every pack he bought, he would give fifty dollars to a beggar. For him, the price of a pack of cigarettes rose monumentally, causing him to stop buying them. By increasing aversion, you can make almost anything unpleasant.

YOU CAN INTENTIONALLY CREATE EMOTIONAL AVERSION IN ORDER TO TURN THE ELEPHANT OFF OF DOING THINGS THAT THE RIDER DOESN'T WANT TO DO.

My colleagues and I have compiled findings about the rider and the elephant, cognitive resources, and habit building, and have created a simple tool for training your willpower muscle on a daily basis that we call the *Habit-list*. Alongside a Personal vision, this is another major tool that will help you fight procrastination.

TOOL: Habit-List

The **Habit-list** is a critical tool for building up your **discipline**. It will help you gradually strengthen your willpower muscle. Although using this method takes only about three minutes a day, it will help you make significant lasting changes in life.

This method can overcome the weakness your neocortex has compared to the strength of the emotional limbic system. The Habit-list incorporates findings from research on self-regulation and cognitive resources as well as *kaizen* techniques and rules for building habits.

A Habit-list can help you learn to wake up early, eat healthily, exercise regularly, focus on education, or learn practically any **positive habit**. It can also be used to control your **bad habits**. It can help you learn to quit smoking, hitting the snooze button, overeating, spending too much time on the Internet, drinking too much, or procrastinating.

Filling in the Habit-list will become a *meta-habit*. What this means is that essentially you will form the habit of learning new habits. The Habit-list is in a way the backbone of personal development, a foundation upon which we can continue to build.

How Does the Habit-List Work?

This method is based on a simple table that you fill in every day. Each table always covers one entire month. Each row represents one day in your life. Each column of the table covers a particular habit: either a good one you would like to pick up, or a bad one you want to get rid of.

You need to give a name to each habit and set a **minimum target**. For example, if you want to wake up earlier, you can call this habit "**waking up**" and set a target of **7:30 a.m.** Setting the bar as low as possible is important so that you, and especially your elephant, don't feel aversion. For example, for **exercising** you can set targets such as **doing 10 push-ups, exercising 5 minutes**, or **running 500 feet**. When objective targets cannot be set for certain habits (such as **eating healthily**), you can use a subjective rating on a scale **from 1 to 10**.

The first column should always cover the habit of filling in the **Habit-list** itself. The last column should contain a rating of **1 to 10**, which should be a subjective evaluation of **how well you lived up to your potential on the given day**. You can include as many habits as you wish. But remember, when it comes to your Habit-list, less is more. For starters, we recommend three to five. Once you have gained more experience with this method, you can add some new habits to the sheet the following month.

To use this method, fill in the corresponding row for each day every evening. For each habit, record your performance, and if you have reached your target, mark that cell with a **green dot**. If you have not met

HABIT-LIST:

HABIT:	HABIT LIST	WAKING UP	EXERCISE: RUNNING	ALCOHOL	...	DAILY POTENTIAL
MIN.:	EVERYDAY	< 7:30 AM	500 FEET	< 2 GLASSES OF WINE		1..10
1.						
2.						
3.					...	
4.						
5.						
⋮					...	

ONE HABIT-LIST IS FOR AN ENTIRE MONTH. EACH ROW IS FOR A NEW DAY. THE COLUMNS CONTAIN HABITS AND BAD HABITS YOU WOULD LIKE TO WORK ON. A TARGET IS SET FOR EACH HABIT THAT DOES NOT ELICIT AVERSION.

your target, mark that cell with a **red dot**. When all your habits for a given day have a green dot next to them, you can put a green dot in the last column where you keep track of how well you have been living up to your potential. If one habit in the row has a red dot, the row in the last column also needs to get a red one.

Usually, the Habit-list begins showing results after just a few days. You can really see big changes though after several weeks. As you begin to form new habits, the Habit-list starts to turn green. When you earn more than twenty green dots in a row, you can begin increasing your performance. Leave your minimum targets unchanged, however, due to possible disruptions.

Ideas for Expanding This Method

- **Blue dots** – If, for reasons beyond your control, you are unable to keep a habit, mark it with a blue dot. For example, if you are sick or on vacation, it is quite clear that you will not be able to do some of the tasks listed in your Habit-list. Use blue dots cautiously. Avoid the potential for *rationalization*.* Blue dots don't count when you evaluate your daily potential.

---

*   *Rationalization* involves looking for rational justification for behaviors that would otherwise be unacceptable. In other words, it is your brain making excuses.

FILLING IN YOUR HABIT-LIST:

HABIT:	HABIT LIST	WAKING UP	EXERCISE: RUNNING	ALCOHOL	•••	DAILY POTENTIAL
MIN.:	EVERYDAY	< 7:30 AM	500 FEET	< 2 GLASSES OF WINE		1..10
1.	YES ●	7:00 AM ●	500 FT ●	0 GL. ●		9 ●
2.	YES ●	7:20 AM ●	500 FT ●	0 GL. ●	•••	7 ●
3.	YES ●	7:00 AM ●	750 FT ●	4 GL. ●		8 ●
4.	YES ●	9:30 AM ●	0 FT ●	0 GL. ●		5 ●
5.	YES ●	7:30 AM ●	500 FT ●	0 GL. ●		7 ●
⋮	⋮	⋮	⋮	⋮	•••	⋮

EVERY EVENING, FILL IN THE ROW FOR THE DAY. FOR EACH HABIT, RECORD YOUR PERFORMANCE, AND IF YOU HAVE MET YOUR TARGET, DRAW A GREEN DOT. IF YOU HAVEN'T, DRAW A RED DOT. PUT A GREEN ONE IN THE LAST COLUMN IF THE ROW IS FULLY GREEN.

- **Non-daily habits** – If you have any habitual tasks that do not need to be done every day (for example, things you do every other day), cross out cells on days you don't need to do them in advance. Once you get to the crossed-out cell, mark it with a green dot.
- **A 30-day challenge** – I recommend picking one habit each month that you will concentrate your efforts on. You want to make sure that you have only green dots for that habit for the entire month. Highlight the name of the habit in your Habit-list in red. You can also use a 30-day challenge to test out whether a certain habit suits you. You might like to try what it's like not drinking alcohol, not eating meat, or taking a cold shower every morning for a month. If you are just beginning to use a Habit-list, I suggest your first 30-day challenge should be filling in the Habit-list itself.
- **Drawing a restart line** – If you don't keep up with your Habit-list—that is, if you end up with too many red dots or if you forget to fill it in for a few days—make a thick black line. Forgive yourself and start over again. The thick black line will help you start over and this time better. Just like with blue dots, be careful not to abuse this. Having two thick lines per month is a bit suspect.

HABIT-LIST - EXTENSIONS:

HABIT:	HABIT LIST	WAKING UP	EXERCISE: RUNNING	EXERCISE: GYM	•••	DAILY POTENTIAL
MIN.:	EVERYDAY	< 7:30 AM	500 FEET	ONCE PER WEEK		1..10
1.	NO ●	7:00 AM ●	0 FT ●	✗ ●		6 ●
2.	NO ●	7:20 AM ●	0 FT ●	✗ ●		5 ●
3.	YES ●	7:00 AM ●	750 FT ●	YES ●		8 ●
4.	YES ●	7:30 AM ●	SICK ●	✗ ●		6 ●
5.	YES ●	7:30 AM ●	SICK ●	✗ ●		7 ●
⋮	⋮	⋮	⋮	⋮	•••	⋮

MARK THE NAME OF YOUR 30-DAY CHALLENGE IN RED AND TRY
TO KEEP THIS HABIT 100%. IF FOR REASONS BEYOND YOUR
CONTROL YOU ARE UNABLE TO DO TO A CERTAIN ACTIVITY, PUT
A BLUE DOT NEXT TO IT. IF A CERTAIN HABIT IS NOT SOMETHING
YOU NEED TO DO EVERY DAY, CROSS OUT THE CELLS IN ADVANCE.
IF YOU HAVEN'T KEPT UP WITH YOUR HABIT-LIST, YOU CAN
RESTART IT BY DRAWING A THICK BLACK LINE.

Why Does the Habit-List Work?

- **Simplicity** – Just like the other methods in this book, this one is very simple too. Simplicity increases the odds of you not putting off using it. A quote attributed to Leonardo da Vinci says, *"Simplicity is the ultimate sophistication."*

- **Regularity** – Being reminded every day of what habits you would like to do will lead you to truly begin working on them and making sure they become lasting ones. Regular reminders help fight against one of the worst things our brains tend to do: forget.

- **Tangibility** – The fact that your Habit-list is written on a piece of paper and is not just in electronic form is crucial. When you have it written down, you create a relationship with it. Even the small effort of clicking a mouse a few times, turning on a computer, or tapping on an app can become barriers that prevent you from using your Habit-list. It is also harder to ignore something that is physically written down, especially when it is sitting on your table or night stand.

- **Visual feedback** – The Habit-list can give you immediate visual feedback. You can see exactly how well you are doing with each habit. At first, it doesn't matter much whether you have green dots or red ones. It is the feedback that is important; the Habit-list is like a mirror. After using this method for several weeks, the number of green dots your Habit-list contains will grow almost automatically; fully green days will begin to appear.

- **Relationship to your vision** – The habits on your Habit-list should correspond to your Personal vision. One of your habits might even be reading your vision every day. You will find this column in my Habit-list. It is important to know why you have each habit: the answer should be contained in your Personal vision.

Potential Risks

- **Overestimating your abilities** – The most frequent mistake people make is that they overestimate their abilities. They set their sights too high, or they try to take on too many new habits at once. Remember, when dealing with a Habit-list, less is more. Be particularly careful when starting out. Take only small manageable bites so that you don't end up choking. Over time, you will discover what targets and how many habits work best for you. This will help you set the bar at the right height.
- **Two no's make never** – If there is one particular habit you leave out, make sure to keep that habit the following day. If you don't, the likelihood of you permanently "burying" it grows significantly.
- **Print your Habit-list a month in advance** – Since each Habit-list covers an entire month, creating a new one is a critical moment. Therefore, you should always prepare yours well in advance. We have created a template that you can use; it is available at **www.procrastination.com/habit-list**. Just to be on the safe side,

you should always have one extra Habit-list printed out. Running out of colored markers (or putting off purchasing them in the first place) might cause similar problems.

- **Rationalization** – Your brain will often look for excuses not to use the Habit-list. Some of the more common ones people come up with are that they don't want to commit themselves to "some table" or that they are afraid that it will limit their creativity. Just the opposite is true. I have clients that are graphic artists and other creative types who use a Habit-list to help improve their creativity. Since it keeps an eye on important parts of your personal development, you have more time, peace and quiet, and even the energy to work on your creative efforts.
- **Procrastinating filling in the Habit-list** – The main risk of this method is when you don't fill in your Habit-list regularly. Filling it in daily is extremely important for achieving success. If you don't fill it in for a given day, mark the first column with a red dot. If you neglect filling it in for some time, it is important to get caught up and fill in the missing rows. If you forget about the Habit-list for more than five days, draw a thick black line and start over as soon as possible. The same idea as for your Personal vision holds true here: don't procrastinate when it comes to fighting procrastination.

I have been using a Habit-list every day for more than three years. It has taught me to wake up early, to take a cold shower in the morning, and

HABIT-LIST INSTRUCTIONS:

1) PRINT IT OUT A MONTH BEFOREHAND (OR PREFERABLY EVEN TWO)
2) DEFINE YOUR HABITS AND SET MINIMUM TARGETS
3) BE CAREFUL OF OVERESTIMATING YOURSELF - MIND YOUR 🐘
4) FILL IN ONE ROW EVERY DAY
5) IF YOU MEET YOUR TARGET, DRAW A GREEN ●
6) IF YOU DON'T, DRAW A RED ●
7) RATE HOW WELL YOU LIVED UP TO YOUR POTENTIAL ON A SCALE OF 1 TO 10
8) THE COLORS OF THE DOTS ARE NOT THAT IMPORTANT, BUT FILLING THE SHEET IN DAILY IS
9) FROM TIME TO TIME, READ YOUR VISION SO YOU KNOW WHY YOU ARE DOING THESE THINGS
10) DON'T PROCRASTINATE WHEN FILLING IN YOUR HABIT-LIST!!!

SOME ADDITIONAL TIPS:

+) IF YOU CAN'T KEEP A HABIT FOR REASONS BEYOND YOUR CONTROL, DRAW A BLUE ●
+) IF SOME HABIT IS NOT A DAILY TASK, CROSS OUT THE CELLS WITH AN ✗
+) PICK ONE HABIT TO FOCUS ON DOING 100% THROUGHOUT A WHOLE MONTH
+) IF YOU FIND YOU HAVE FORGOTTEN ABOUT YOUR BULLY-SHEET, RESTART

...AND ONE MORE THING...BUY SOME MARKERS ● ● ●

to exercise. Thanks to it, I regularly repeat my Personal vision to myself, and I know why I want to live every day to the fullest.

Once, I took a 30-day challenge and tried to cut out alcohol for a full month. It was quite an interesting experiment. I had incomparably more energy than before when I used to drink a few glasses of wine in my favorite bar before bed. Today, thanks to what I learned from this experience, I hardly drink at all.

My Habit-list has trained me to read and watch educational videos every day; it has changed my diet and taught me to plan out my tasks for each and every day. I can even say that without it I would have never finished this book and that my company wouldn't exist. Thanks to my Habit-list, I have my elephant under control like never before.

Decision Paralysis

During one consultation session, the director of a relatively large company told me that she would often sit at work doing nothing at all. She didn't know where to start. She had so many tasks that just choosing one completely exhausted her; instead she would rather go and water the office plants.

Another one of my clients had over one thousand unopened e-mails in his inbox. Whenever he logged into his e-mail, all his energy was drained from him. Later, he missed this energy for other more important tasks. In both of these cases, ineffectiveness and procrastination were the results of **decision paralysis**.

The paralysis that results from having too many options to choose from is, besides a lack of self-regulation, the second main reason for low effectiveness and productivity. If you want to fight procrastination, you need to learn how to cope with decision paralysis over the long term.

Every day you are faced with many decisions to make. Making up your mind can be so difficult that you tire yourself out. Decision-making, just like unpleasant tasks, drains your cognitive resources and wears out your willpower muscle.[61] It can get so tired that you have no energy left to do any actual work. When deciding between doing two important things—say, task A or task B—people have the tendency to either do nothing or to choose to do a trivial task C.

The more choices you have and the more different they are, the greater the paralysis you will experience. Choosing one e-mail out of ten isn't as hard as picking one out of a thousand. The act of choosing elicits in you, or rather in your elephant, the same type of aversion as if you had to do a large and complicated task. This is why you put off making a decision. When you put off making choices, you also put off doing related activities that are based on these decisions.

An extensive study of the clients of one of America's largest insurance companies discovered that the more retirement saving options there were, the fewer people actually saved for their retirement.[62] When people have more choices, it is less likely that they will be able to pick one retirement savings plan.

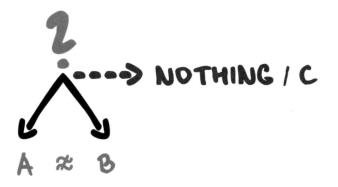

NOTHING / C

A ≉ B

WHEN PEOPLE HAVE TO CHOOSE BETWEEN TWO IMPORTANT BUT HARDLY COMPARABLE OPTIONS - OPTIONS A AND B - THEY HAVE THE TENDENCY TO PICK NOTHING AT ALL OR FOCUS ON A TRIVIAL OPTION C.

For every 10 new options on the market, the amount of people investing in some type of plan drops by about 2%. With 5 options available, 70.1% of people are able to make a decision; however, when there are 15 to choose from, only 67.7% can make up their mind, and when there are 35 options, a mere 63% of people are able to pick a savings plan. Nonetheless, the general trend on the market is for the number of retirement savings plans to multiply. The resulting decision paralysis means that many people have stopped saving entirely.

In another interesting study, a group of several hundred doctors were presented with the case of a patient who had hip problems.[63] According to the scenario presented by the researchers, the patient's doctor had already tried all possible medications on him but to no avail. Therefore, the patient had been referred to a specialist for a total hip replacement.

Then the researchers told two different versions of the story to two groups of doctors. In the first version, the doctors were told that the patient's doctor had forgotten to try **one type of medication** on him. The doctors were then asked what they would do in light of this new information. In this situation, 72% cancelled the referral and had the patient try the medicine.

The second version was very similar; the only difference was that the doctors were told there were **two different medications** that the patient's doctor had forgotten to try. Once again, the doctors were asked what they would do. In this second scenario, 47% of doctors let the patient go to

DECISION PARALYSIS - RESEARCH:

1:

72% vs. 28%

THE MORE DIFFICULT A DECISION
IS TO MAKE, THE LESS LIKELY IT
IS THAT YOU WILL MAKE ONE.
ADDING ONE MORE MEDICINE
TO CHOOSE FROM SIGNIFICANTLY
INCREASED THE NUMBER OF
DOCTORS WHO SENT A PATIENT
FOR AN OPERATION.

2:

53% vs. 47%

surgery. Having to choose between two types of medication made the decision-making process more difficult. As a result, the number of doctors that put off making any decision at all increased with the consequence that the patient had to go through the operation.

Decision paralysis is treacherous not only because it makes decision-making difficult. Problems can arise even if you do manage to choose one option out of many. The odds are higher that you will later regret your decision.[64]

The fact that other options exist leads you into thinking what it would have been like if you had chosen differently. Thinking about other possible choices makes you less and less happy with the decision you have actually made; naturally, if you are picking a college, a job, or a life partner, this is not an ideal situation to be in.

Another research study focused on how much people regret their decisions. In this experiment, researchers put out an advertisement for a photography course.[65] During the course, students took many pictures and at the end were told that they could develop their two favorite ones.

Once they were developed, the students were told they could only take one home. One group of participants was told they had to choose immediately and that in **the future they could not change their minds**. The second group was offered the option of being **able to change their decisions at a future time**; they could return the picture they had chosen and take home the other one. Researchers measured how happy the students were with their photographs in both groups.

It was found that when the students had the opportunity to change their decisions, they were significantly less happy with the photograph they had chosen. On the other hand, those who could not change their minds were significantly happier with their choice.

Another part of the study tested how well people could predict their future happiness. A different group of students was told they needed to select which course they would rather attend. In the first course, students could choose only one photograph and would not be able to change their minds while the second course offered them the possibility of changing their minds.

Since people have a tendency to leave the back door open, most students selected the second course. As the first part of the experiment demonstrated, at the end of this scenario, people were significantly less satisfied.

This study shows why it is a good idea to intentionally close the scissors of potential with the help of your personal vision and to choose only opportunities that you are able to fully commit yourself to.

How can you put information about the causes of decision paralysis to use in real life? How can you overcome it and increase your effectiveness and productivity?

In order to fight this problem, you need to learn the art of consciously minimizing the amount of decisions you need to make on a daily basis.

When you really must make a decision, you need to simplify and systematize the process as much as possible.

What tasks will help you most fulfill your personal vision? When selecting tasks, it is always a good idea to think about how they relate to your vision. It is also worth using a task management system that will help you even more with paralysis.

Most time management tools, however, do not take decision paralysis into account. They utilize lists of tasks that you must pick from again and again throughout the day. This is why we have created a method we call *To-Do today* that will help you plan each and every day so that decision paralysis doesn't drain you. Besides your **Personal vision** and **Habit-list**, **To-Do today** is a third key tool you can use to bring an end to procrastination.

TOOL: To-Do Today

Occasionally, I work with people who are on the edge of burning out. A project manager once described to me his situation: he had to do more tasks than he had time for. New tasks kept popping up faster than he had time to process them. This caused pressure, which resulted in a high level of stress. This stress led to poor sleeping habits and subsequently a lack of energy and the inability to deal with tasks effectively.

He told me that he felt like a dung beetle rolling an ever-growing ball of feces in front of him. His ball of problems had grown so large that it was literally crushing him into the ground.

WHEN YOU DON'T DEAL WITH PROBLEMS, THEY HAVE A TENDENCY TO BALL UP TO THE POINT THAT THEY CRUSH YOU.

During our sessions, my client learned how to use the **To-Do today** method, which helped him get the most important and urgent tasks done every day. Over time, he was able to limit new tasks and learned how to delegate those that were not necessary for him to do.

BY GETTING THE MOST IMPORTANT TASKS DONE EVERY DAY, LIMITING NEW TASKS, AND DELEGATING SOME TASKS TO OTHERS, YOU CAN BEGIN CHIPPING AWAY AT YOUR BALL OF PROBLEMS.

One month after our first meeting, a changed man showed up in my office. He told me how much better he was sleeping and how his days had acquired a sense of order that enabled him to do triple the things he could before.

The To-Do today method can fundamentally increase your **productivity** and **effectiveness**. Using this method will help you overcome the driving forces of low discipline. It will help you fight against decision paralysis and will lower your elephant's aversion to performing large and complicated tasks. Overall, this tool will not only increase the odds of you actually getting to work on your tasks, but it will also positively affect the likelihood of you completing them as well.

In order to manage their tasks, people often use various lists, tools, or even comprehensive methods (like GTD or ZTD*). Over the years we tried more than a hundred tools, programs, and apps, and we selected their best aspects, which we have simplified and joined together with current findings from the fields of neuroscience, human motivation, and effectiveness. This is how we developed the To-Do today method.

The main distinguishing aspect of our method is that **it does not use lists**; instead it uses visual *mind maps*, which present clearly and visually the information you need. Since the visual cortex is the most developed part of the human brain, this method is more natural for our brains.

---

*   **GTD** = Getting Things Done from David Allen's book of the same name.

    ZTD = Zen to Done from Leo Babaut's book of the same name.

The linear arrangement of a list makes it less effective at emphasizing relationships between tasks, priorities, and temporal links. There are several other disadvantages to lists. People have a tendency to make them too long. The result is an aversion, which increases the chances of procrastination. Long lists also contribute to decision paralysis. Thus, people would often rather hide their lists away or perhaps even stop using them at all. To-Do today overcomes those flaws of lists.

How can you increase the number of tasks you complete? How can you decrease task aversion and paralysis? How can you learn to plan your entire day and as a result gain a better sense of peace?

To-Do today is a comprehensive tool you can use for everyday task management. You can either adopt it completely or you can use its principles to inspire and improve the system you already use.

How Does To-Do Today Work?

The following ten guidelines will significantly increase the amount of tasks you are able to handle on a daily basis. These principles can help you live every day to its fullest without frightening your elephant, evoking decision paralysis, or experiencing exhaustion at the end of the day.

- **Lay out your tasks** – Take a blank piece of paper and randomly write down all of the tasks you would like to do on a given day.
- **Give each task a concrete and pleasant name** – You will be better able to imagine what the task requires and thus decrease your aversion towards it. For example, labeling a task "Call the mechanic"

LISTS AREN'T IDEAL FOR PLANNING TASKS. THE LONGER
THEY ARE, THE BIGGER THE AVERSION YOU HAVE AND
THE MORE THEY CONTRIBUTE TO DECISION PARALYSIS.

does not evoke the same negative feelings as the too abstract "Mechanic" might. If you are able to imagine your task, you will eliminate fear of the unknown and uncertainty.

- **Split large tasks up and combine small ones together** – Each task should take you between 30 and 60 minutes to complete. If you have to do something more complicated (such as "Writing a book"), always break it up into a set of smaller tasks ("Write two paragraphs of the book"). Large and complicated tasks frighten your elephant, and therefore you avoid them. By breaking large tasks up, you will be able to significantly decrease the aversion you might have towards them. Thus, you decrease the odds of procrastinating.

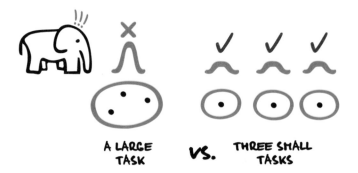

A LARGE TASK **VS.** THREE SMALL TASKS

LARGE TASKS ELICIT GREATER AVERSION THAN SMALL ONES. THEREFORE, IT'S WORTH LEARNING HOW TO BREAK LARGE MOUTHFULS INTO BITE-SIZED PIECES.

Very small tasks ("Write one e-mail") should be combined into one larger task ("Write all e-mails" or "Write 20 most important e-mails"). By batch processing of related tasks, you will not have to shift your attention between different activities so often, and thus you will not disrupt your flow during the day.

- **Color code your priorities** – Draw a red circle around the tasks that are of highest priority (those that are important and urgent), draw a blue circle around those that are of medium priority (those that are important but are not yet urgent), and then draw a green circle around those that are of the lowest priority (those that if you don't do, the world won't end, but which would still be nice to complete as a bonus).

- **Define your path for the day** – Link together your tasks with arrows; the path you make should follow the best order for completing your tasks. At the start of the day when your cognitive resources are still fresh, begin with the most difficult and high-priority tasks. Try to follow difficult tasks with less demanding ones and creative tasks with more routine ones. The "path" you create is critical for fighting decision paralysis. You won't have to spend time during the day thinking about what you should be working on.

- **Make time estimates** – Try to plan certain times for each task; define when you will start working on it and when you want to finish it. You should stick to these times, just as you would if you had an important appointment with someone. At first, your estimates won't be exact, but with more experience they will get better. By defining an exact time to start an activity, you have improved the odds that you will really start. After all, as they say, *"Starting really is half the battle."*

- **Focus on the one thing only** – Once you start working on a task, concentrate only on that activity. You may switch your e-mail notifications off, put your phone on silent mode, or ask your co-workers not to disturb you. Clean your work area so that you limit distractions. By focusing on one task, you will find your state of flow more easily, and thanks to the peace you have created nothing will disrupt it.

- **Learn when to stop** – Once you finish a task, cross it out and symbolically bring the task to a close. Some people have problems not only starting tasks but also finishing them. The first time you hold in your hands a completely crossed out To-Do today, you will understand how important this step is.

- **Replenish your cognitive resources** – Plan short breaks in between tasks so you can restore your energy. Once you get to an arrow, do something that will renew your willpower muscle. Go for a short walk around the block, or head out to the park. Drink some fresh juice, or increase your blood sugar by eating a piece of fruit. Let your brain rest a bit. If you have been doing a creative task, do something with your hands. Your breaks can last only several minutes, but they will help you maintain your concentration and energy until the evening. Don't take a rest only when you feel the need to do so. Take breaks regularly throughout the day as a preventive measure.

- **Make a habit out of creating a To-Do today** – It would be ideal if you could prepare your To-Do today every evening for the following day. You will see how much better you will sleep knowing that you have the next day all planned out. It is also possible to prepare it as the first thing in the morning. The last item on your To-Do today could be "Prepare To-Do today for tomorrow" or "Fill in the Habit-list." Or you can even include preparing your To-Do today as one of the items on your Habit-list. This way you will ensure that you will not forget to make it.

Why Does To-Do Today Work?

- **Tangibility and simplicity** – Just like your Habit-list and your Personal vision, your To-Do today is written on paper. In order to overcome procrastination, it is very important that the methods you use are as simple as possible. Therefore, the To-Do today method has been stripped of any unneeded elements. Unnecessary complexity causes aversion. As Antoine de Saint-Exupéry once said, *"Perfection is achieved, not when there is nothing more to add, but when there is nothing left to take away."*

- **Visual arrangement** – By color coding your priorities, one look will be enough to let you know what awaits you during the day. The visual path will eliminate decision paralysis. If you place your To-Do today on your desk, you will know what you are supposed to do and when, just by looking at it.

- **Head cleaning** – By committing your tasks to paper, you will relieve your brain. You can hold about six thoughts in your working memory.[66] If this space is taken up by tasks, you will not be able to use your full mental capacity to work effectively and think creatively.

Potential Risks

- **Overestimating your abilities** – When you are new to the To-Do today method, you should start out with just four to five tasks per day. It is better to plan fewer tasks and actually do them than to plan more and not manage them at all. In time, you will discover the optimal amount of tasks for you.

- **Wrong time estimation** – When you schedule your tasks, make sure to set aside some extra time. If you finish a task earlier than expected, take a short break and then begin working on your next task ahead of time. If you finish a task later than expected, once again take a short break before starting in on your next task. It may be that at first you won't be able to correctly determine how much time each task will take. No worries. The more experience you gain, the better your time planning will become.
- **New task** – If an urgent task arises during the day, you can deal with it immediately (if something is on fire, put it out), or you can take a detour on your To-Do today map. In the worst case, you can create a new To-Do today. It will take you only a few minutes, but you will be more effective for the rest of the day.

Ideas for Expanding This Method

- **First thing in the morning** – Since your cognitive resources are fullest at the start of the day, we recommend the first task on your To-Do today to be the most important one (and perhaps the most unpleasant one to complete). Once you have completed this task, everything else you do that day will seem easy in comparison.

- **Two paths** – If some of your tasks require you to wait for other people or if you handle unexpected tasks, we recommend you to mark two independent paths on your To-Do today. The second path does not need to include exact times, and you can work on each task as the situation allows. Therefore, if your first path cannot be followed because, for example, you are waiting for other people, you will have a plan B.

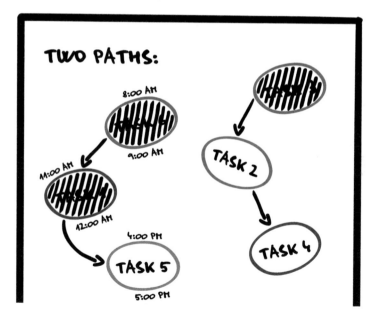

To-Do Today, Ideas, and Calendar

You can use the To-Do today method by itself, or you can use it as part of a more extensive system. You can add a part that is called *To-Do*. It contains all tasks that are not on the order of the day. To-Do is like a storehouse that holds all of the tasks you have to do in the future. It looks very similar to To-Do today, the only differences being that it may consist of multiple sheets of paper, the tasks it contains does not need to be connected by arrows, and times and priorities do not need to be indicated.

The second component you can add is called *Ideas*. It contains your ideas—things that you don't want to forget about but which at the same time don't belong on your To-Do today or To-Do. This part is useful for capturing all of your essential ideas in one place so that you don't need to keep "rediscovering" them.

The last part of this system is a classic *calendar* that only contains time-bound tasks such as appointments and other scheduled events.

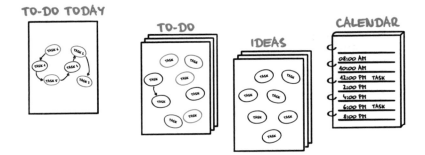

Whenever you create a new To-Do today, you should select tasks from your To-Do, ideas or calendar that you want to accomplish during the upcoming day. All tasks you have transferred to your To-Do today should be crossed out from the paper they were initially on. Thus, in this system, every task should be contained in just one place.

CREATING **THE TO-DO TODAY:**

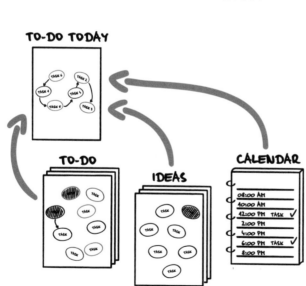

How Can You Deal With New Tasks?

If **a new task** pops up during the day, there are several ways you can handle it:

- **Deal with it immediately** – If a new task is extremely important (if something is on fire), take care of it immediately (put it out). You should also immediately deal with any tasks that you can complete very quickly, e.g., within a minute.

- **Put it on your To-Do today** – If the task is so urgent and important that you must deal with it in the present day, add it to your To-Do today.

- **Put it on your To-Do** – If the task doesn't need to be done today, add it to your To-Do and take care of it in the future.

- **Write it in your calendar** – If your task is scheduled (such as a meeting), write it in your calendar.

- **Add it to your ideas** – Another option is that some tasks are not so important, but you would still prefer not to forget about them. Include these tasks on your ideas.

- **Delegate** – For every new task, you should think about the suitability of delegating it to someone else.

- **Throw it away** – If a task doesn't belong in any of these categories, you can sometimes throw it in the "trash bin" without any regret. The art of saying "no" is an important skill for developing long-term mental welfare.

DEALING WITH NEW TASKS:

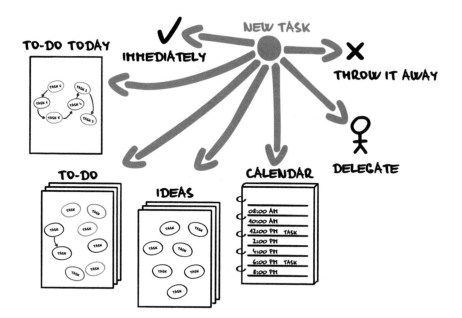

TO-DO TODAY INSTRUCTIONS:

1) TAKE A PIECE OF PAPER AND WRITE ALL OF THE TASKS YOU WANT TO DO ON THAT DAY
2) GIVE EACH TASK A CLEAR AND PLEASANT NAME
3) BREAK BIG TASKS INTO SMALLER ONES; GROUP SMALL TASKS INTO BIG ONES
4) COLOR CODE THE PRIORITIES OF YOUR TASKS ● ● ●
5) MAKE A PATH CONNECTING YOUR TASKS IN THE ORDER YOU WANT TO DO THEM
6) SET THE TIMES WHEN YOU WANT TO START AND FINISH EACH TASK
7) ONCE YOU START AN ACTIVITY, FOCUS ON NOTHING ELSE
8) ONCE YOU HAVE COMPLETED A TASK, CROSS IT OUT
9) TAKE A BREAK IN BETWEEN TASKS TO REGENERATE YOUR COGNITIVE RESOURCES
10) MAKE A DAILY HABIT OUT OF CREATING A TO-DO-TODAY MIND MAP!!!

ADDITIONAL TIPS:

+) DO THE MOST UNPLEASANT TASK FIRST THING IN THE MORNING
+) YOU CAN CREATE TWO PATHS; IF YOU GET STUCK ON ONE, USE THE OTHER
+) YOU CAN USE TO-DO TODAY ALONE OR TOGETHER WITH TO-DO, IDEAS, AND CALENDAR

...JUST TO BE SURE, ADD USING TO-DO-TODAY TO YOUR HABIT-LIST

You now have the three main tools it takes to fight procrastination effecitively. A **Personal vision** will give you motivation. A **Habit-list** will help you get your elephant under control and strengthen your willpower muscle. A **To-Do today** will help you to get rid of decision paralysis and to move you forward every day. Your productivity and effectiveness will increase significantly. For these tools to work as best they can, you need to learn another critical skill: knowing how to step out of your *comfort zone...*

The Comfort Zone of the Masses: The Birthplace of Evil

I read in the newspaper that one of the most influential psychologists, Professor Philip Zimbardo, whose studies and books have greatly inspired our work, was coming to town. As soon as I found out that he would be visiting, I knew we needed to meet in person. My colleagues and I overcame our initial unpleasant emotions and wrote him to set up a meeting.

By this overcoming of ourselves we unknowingly did something that we ended up talking about with Professor Zimbardo throughout our entire meeting. The information we obtained from him was so fundamental that it stimulated me to significantly improve my personal vision. Zimbardo taught us how to form a habit of becoming an **everyday hero**.

What goes through the heads of bad people? How would you behave if you were a prison guard? Why do some people behave viciously but some act like heroes? Philip Zimbardo has been dedicated to answering these questions his entire life. His work has shown that the average originally good person can be influenced by his or her surroundings to do very bad things. It doesn't matter if we are talking about the father of a family, a strongly religious person, or an otherwise upstanding citizen.

In his famous, yet slightly controversial **Stanford prison experiment**, Zimbardo selected a group of volunteers and then he chose the most average and healthy individuals out of them. In a mock basement prison, he assigned half the participants the role of guards and half the role of inmates.[67] What happened was that after only a few days, the guards began to treat the prisoners very cruelly; the imprisoned participants were humiliated, psychologically abused, and subjected to horrible, yet well-thought-out punishments. As a result, the experiment had to be stopped prematurely.

As a psychologist, Zimbardo has also dealt with the **Abu Ghraib** prison abuse case. In this real prison in Iraq, Iraqis were the prisoners and American soldiers were the guards. Here too, the guards exhibited extremely cruel behavior towards the prisoners. However, since this was not a controlled experiment, the situation did not come to an end after a few days. At Abu Ghraib, evil grew out of control for a hellishly long time.[68]

What makes people turn evil in these situations? Zimbardo's research demonstrates how great the influence of *herd mentality* can be.[69] People do things because other people are doing them. They don't want to be exposed to the social pressure and discomfort that would arise if they leave the herd.

Thus, people aren't often evil themselves; they are just unable to leave the evil herd or to rebel against it. As a quote attributed to Albert Einstein says: *"The world will not be destroyed by those who do evil, but by those who watch them without doing anything."*

The herd effect is why some homeless people remain homeless. They are afraid that if they tried to find a job their homeless peers would view them as traitors.

EVIL →

PEOPLE AREN'T PRIMARILY EVIL. EVIL BEHAVIOR
IS A SECONDARY CONSEQUENCE OF THE FACT
THAT THEY DON'T HAVE THE COURAGE TO LEAVE
THE EVIL CROWD.

For many people, abandoning the crowd is so unpleasant that they will follow it wherever it goes, even if it is headed straight to hell. Sometimes all it takes is for someone with authority to do something and the herd will follow. Those who are unable to leave the herd become accomplices to evil. The philosopher Edmund Burke had this to say about the risks of becoming a passive member of the herd: *"The only thing necessary for the triumph of evil is for good men to do nothing."*

How is it that every once in a while someone appears who manages to leave the herd and point out its flaws? How is it possible that some people stop to help when they see a car accident while others just drive by? Leaving the herd is one manifestation of the ability that Zimbardo calls **heroism**.

During the Stanford prison experiment, a hero emerged from amongst Zimbardo's colleagues. It was she who stepped out from the crowd when the experiment got out of hand and forced Zimbardo to stop it. This woman would later go on to become Zimbardo's wife, by the way.

In Abu Ghraib, a young soldier became a hero; despite the risks, he managed to break away from the herd and reported what was going on in the prison.

At our meeting, Zimbardo explained to us that everyone can train their heroism; you can gradually build it up. His research has shown that heroes aren't born: they are made over time.[70]

TOOL: Heroism

Although the word "heroism" is usually reserved for extraordinary acts, it is appropriate to use it to describe a skill that you can use every day. The courage to jump onto the subway tracks to save someone's life and the ability to overcome procrastination are both built on the same foundation. It is only a different level of the skill of **intentionally stepping out of your comfort zone**.[71]

Every one of us has comfort zones. Those zones can be either **physical**, such as a warm bed in the morning, or **social**, such as being part of a crowd and doing the same thing as everyone else.

Most of the important things you need to do to fulfill your personal vision are not located in your comfort zone, but outside its boundaries. They are in the zones of discomfort. As Albert Einstein is attributed to have said: *"The one who follows the crowd will usually go no further than the crowd. Those who walk alone are likely to find themselves in places no one has ever been before."*

If you want to get up in the morning, you need to switch off the alarm clock and get out of your bed. If you want to help someone who has been in an accident, you need to stop your car, get out, and start acting. If you want to get to know someone, the first thing you need to do is strike up a conversation. If you want to have your own business, you need to be able to set up business meetings. If you want to live life meaningfully and to the fullest, you need to know how to stop procrastinating.

Thanks to hedonic adaptation you will get used to any comfort zone. Even if you crawl into the most comfortable bed in the world, after a few days of lazing about you will stop enjoying it. Therefore, going outside your comfort zone is an important step towards reaching happiness. If you learn to overcome yourself, your brain's reward center will be activated more often and more dopamine will be released.[72]

HEROISM

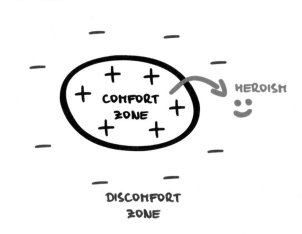

HEROISM IS AN EXPRESSION OF YOUR ABILITY TO LEAVE YOUR COMFORT ZONE. IF YOU SUCCEED IN DOING SO, YOU ARE REWARDED WITH RELEASED DOPAMINE.

Learning to be a hero is another key to increasing **discipline**. Heroism is what we call a *microhabit*. The difference between a habit and a microhabit is that a habit refers to something you do once a day, whereas a microhabit is something that you should always have on your mind. The more capable of Heroism you become, the less you will procrastinate, and therefore you will be able to better live up to your personal vision.

How Can You Train Yourself to Become More Heroic?

At our meeting, Zimbardo took one of my markers and drew a big black dot on his forehead. He wanted to demonstrate to us an easy method for training Heroism. If you spend all day with the black dot on your forehead—walking around, taking the bus, shopping, talking with people—it will slowly stop bothering you that people are looking at you strangely. You will get used to being different. Unpleasant social pressure will slowly decrease. You will get used to stepping out of your social comfort zone and learn how to stand out from the herd. Zimbardo explained to us that heroes are always sort of **deviants**.

Zimbardo's hero is not overly influenced by those around him or her. He is able to stand out from the crowd and be the first person to take action. Heroes have the ability to be different because they have trained themselves to be used to this feeling. The odds are that these types of people will stop when they see an accident to provide help while all others, in keeping with the herd, just drive by.

True heroism occurs when nobody is around. Most procrastination usually takes place behind closed doors. In order to defeat it, you need to learn how to be a hero in front of yourself. It's not for nothing they say *"Our character is what we do when no one is looking."*

Since Heroism is a microhabit, it is good to have it on your mind at all times. It might even be a good idea to make stepping out of your comfort zone into a sort of passion.

How can you do this? Whenever you have the chance, try to step outside your comfort zone. Give yourself orders and follow them. So, start up that conservation with the stranger sitting next to you on the bus. Even though you don't feel like doing anything in particular, set about doing the most unpleasant thing for you in the given situation.

Once you have a chance to be a hero, seize it, and follow the **three-second rule** of the samurai.[73] Take action within five heartbeats. If you start thinking too much, your brain will have a tendency to come up with rationalizations justifying why you should stay in your comfort zone.

You can train being an everyday hero using the **first thing in the morning** method presented in the To-Do today chapter. If the first task you do every morning is the most unappealing one, it will encourage you to act heroically throughout the entire day. For example, I practice being a morning hero by exercising right after I get up, followed by an uncomfortable cold shower.

PETR LUDWIG AND PHILIP ZIMBARDO

When you gradually train the skill of Heroism, you will increase the number of crucial actions that you actually take in your life. Being a hero is one of the most important preconditions for living your life to the fullest. Philip Zimbardo summarized it: *"The core of your life can be reduced to two types of actions: those taken and those not taken."*

Heroism is the fourth important tool contained in this book. Along with your **Personal vision**, **Habit-list**, and **To-Do today**, it creates an interlinked group of methods for fighting procrastination.

Here is an example of how these tools might work together: Your vision tells you what kind of habits should be on your Habit-list and what kind of tasks should be on your To-Do today. Your Habit-list can include items such as "read my vision" or "create To-Do today." The last To-Do today task might be filling in your Habit-list. Finally, Heroism increases the odds of fully utilizing the other methods.

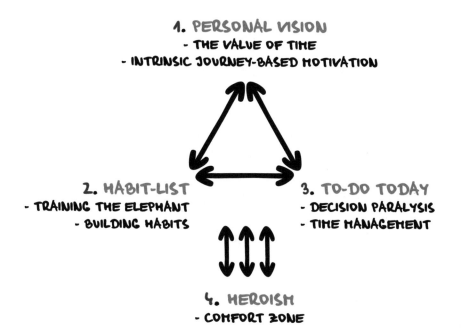

1. PERSONAL VISION
- THE VALUE OF TIME
- INTRINSIC JOURNEY-BASED MOTIVATION

2. HABIT-LIST
- TRAINING THE ELEPHANT
- BUILDING HABITS

3. TO-DO TODAY
- DECISION PARALYSIS
- TIME MANAGEMENT

4. HEROISM
- COMFORT ZONE

Chapter Recap: Discipline

The main cause of procrastination is an inability to **self-regulate**—the skill of giving yourself orders and following them.

The inability to follow orders stems from the fact that your rational neocortex (**your rider**) is often giving them but that your older and stronger emotional limbic system (**your elephant**) isn't listening.

Self-regulation is dependent on your **cognitive resources**, your imaginary willpower muscle, which expresses the current energy of your rider. Throughout the day you can replenish these resources and you can also increase their capacity over the long term.

In order to **replenish** your cognitive resources, you should take regularly scheduled breaks throughout the day: take a five-minute walk, eat some fruit, or drink a glass of fresh juice. To **strengthen** these resources, you need to gradually learn new habits.

The **Habit-list** tool will enable you to work daily on your habits and at the same time to break the bad ones. It is important to use the **kaizen** approach: small steps lead to big changes.

Decision paralysis, along with a lack of self-regulation, is the second main deplenisher of your cognitive resources. The less often you are forced to make decisions during the day, the more energy you will have for completing tasks.

To-Do today will help you plan out each and every day, label priorities, times, and the order in which you will complete the tasks you want to do. It will help you significantly decrease decision paralysis during the course of the day.

You can expand To-Do today with other useful parts such as the **To-Do**, **Ideas**, and a classic **calendar**. Together they create an integrated task and time-management system.

By training the microhabit of **Heroism** you can learn to step outside of your social and physical **comfort zones**. If you can leave your comfort zone, the odds of you living your life to the fullest will increase.

Discipline is overall a skill that helps you to take steps towards fulfilling your personal vision. Thus, discipline is the opposite of procrastination.

Here you can once again evaluate your **discipline** and your use of related tools. I recommend regular re-evaluation. You will find that the higher you rate your use of your **Habit-list**, the **To-Do today**, and **Heroism**, the greater your discipline will be.

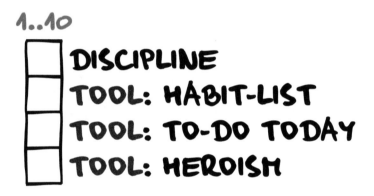

1..10

- [ ] DISCIPLINE
- [ ] TOOL: HABIT-LIST
- [ ] TOOL: TO-DO TODAY
- [ ] TOOL: HEROISM

OUTCOMES

HOW TO FIND HAPPINESS
AND ALSO KEEP IT

Once I met with a longtime colleague in a cafe. He had recently recovered from having his appendix removed and confided in me that he had hit rock bottom emotionally. He told me: "Everything is meaningless. I am just going to quit and go get an administrative job somewhere." In the end we agreed that before he made any decisions we should meet again and calmly go over everything. I had my suspicions. All signs pointed to the fact that my colleague had caught a pretty bad *hamster* (see page 178).

Perhaps we have all at one time or another thought about the recipe for happiness. Studies on hedonic adaptation have shown that the key to happiness can't be found in any material possessions or goals, but instead in the journey—in the process of fulfilling your personal vision.[74] If you spend every day doing meaningful things at which you are skilled, you will achieve a state of flow. Flow will help you reach desired **outcomes**, both emotional and material, more often.

On the one hand, such activities stimulate the brain's reward centers, which then release dopamine—now we are talking about **emotional outcomes**. On the other, once you meet your established milestones and can see the real results of your work, you will have achieved **material outcomes**.

VISION + ACTIONS = OUTCOMES

Even though you may be making daily progress towards fulfilling your vision, sometimes things will throw you off, leaving you suddenly unhappy. Negative external influences, failure, and reliving unpleasant experiences from the past are the most frequent factors that put people off track. Sometimes people become unhappy just due to mere chemical changes in the brain with no apparent external cause.[75] You might find yourself getting off track if you spend a long time not doing things that get you in the state of flow.

EVEN THOUGH YOU DO MEANINGFUL THINGS THAT MAKE YOU HAPPY, SOMETIMES YOU WILL BE THROWN OFF TRACK AND BECOME UNHAPPY.

I began to suspect that the reason for my off-track colleague's un-happiness was a lack of flow. For quite some time, he would lie by himself at home; he stopped providing consultations and training to his clients, and spent no time in the company of others. Since he is a very social person, this sucked him dry emotionally. A few days after we spoke, a smile had returned to his face. What had caused him to restart?

In this chapter you will learn about the *Inner-switch* technique, which will help you turn negative feelings into positive ones. It is a tool that can even help you overcome depressive states and get back to being happy. Another one of our tools, the *Flow-list*, will help you maintain lasting happiness. The last thing we cover is the *Hamster-restart button*, which will help you reboot your entire personal-development system if something sends you flying way off track.

By using the tools contained in this chapter, you will become more **emotionally balanced**, and you will be able to live up to your potential more effectively. Happy people, you see, procrastinate less.

Where Do Negative Emotions Come From?

The *amygdala* is one of the oldest parts of the human brain. It is the part of the brain that searches out danger in everything we perceive.[76] When hundreds of thousands of years ago our ancestors heard grass rustling in the savannah, it was the amygdala that assessed the potential risk and set off the alarm in the form of a strong negative emotion and they started to run away. The amygdala acts as an early warning detector, and one of its main jobs is to increase our chances of survival.[77]

As far as survival is concerned, it is no big deal if your amygdala makes a mistake and sets off a false alarm. It would be a far bigger problem if it didn't react to actual danger. If our prehistoric ancestor took off running by mistake, it was better for his survival than if he hadn't reacted at all and was attacked by a predator.

So that our brains don't ignore potential dangers, the amygdala has evolved to have a greater tendency to emphasize possible risks.[78] Today this characteristic of our brain is played upon by the media. There is a reason why most news you read about in the papers and see on television is delivered negatively. Thanks to the stronger response of the amygdala to potential risks, negative news can catch significantly more of your attention.

Thanks to the constant bombardment of our amygdalae, many people today are awash in a shower of negative information. Their brains are gradually trained to notice mainly negative news, and they start to ignore

THE AMYGDALA RESPONDS STRONGLY TO NEGATIVE STIMULI. IF THERE ARE MANY OF THEM, YOU WILL BEGIN TO IGNORE POSITIVE ONES. THIS WILL MAKE YOU GRADUALLY LESS HAPPY.

the positive news. They are becoming "learned pessimists" who are constantly more and more unhappy.

Negative people often inadvertently spread their emotions to the people around them. Just take a look at an average pub on a Friday evening. You will see people complaining in unison about how all politicians lie, nothing works, and everything is terrible.*

Negative emotions are more socially contagious than positive ones as a result of the function of the amygdala. They spread from person to person easily. As they spread to more and more people, they will eventually find their way back to their source. The result is a **feedback loop** and negative emotions are even strengthened.

---

* *Author's note:* Sometimes I suspect that some people's personal vision is to complain. Since these people have mastered their negativity to the point of perfection, perhaps in the process of complaining they catch their flow. But complaining won't change anything by itself, and it usually just makes the situation worse.

UNHAPPINESS IS SOCIALLY CONTAGIOUS. AS IT SPREADS TO OTHER PEOPLE, IT WILL EVENTUALLY COME BACK TO THE ORIGINAL SOURCE, CREATING A FEEDBACK LOOP.

Although we most likely live in the greatest time of abundance in history,* negative emotions might be so infectious that some people are drowning in a sea of worry and actually start to believe that everything is wrong. Collective pessimism makes them vulnerable to falling victim to *learned helplessness*, which is often the cause of depression.[79]

---

* *Author's note:* For more than 100 billion people[80] that have lived on the Earth before us, drinkable tap water, accessible healthcare, education, and technology that we nowadays have, were never such a sure thing. Although our world isn't perfect and has its problems, in comparison to other periods in history we are in many ways incomparably much better off.

How can you resist being infected by negative emotions? How can you avoid the loop of learned helplessness? How can you make better use of the advantages of today's world? What steps can you take to not only become happy, but stay that way?

First, you will discover how the loop of learned helplessness originates and then you will learn to overcome it. To deal with it you will have to consciously switch your focus from negative stimuli to positive ones.

IF YOU LEARN HOW TO REORIENT YOUR FOCUS FROM NEGATIVE STIMULI TO POSITIVE ONES, YOU WILL BECOME HAPPIER.

Cycle of Learned Helplessness

Martin Seligman's research demonstrates that just a few negative stimuli can convince you that everything is bad and there is nothing you can do about it.[81] Due to this conviction, a feeling of helplessness can overcome you, which can lead to depression and life resignation.

In one experiment they put a rodent into a box (imagine, for example, a hamster), and then placed a transparent cover on the box.[82] The hamster tried to get out. The first day it jumped and jumped but kept hitting its head on the cover. The second day its attempts at escape were more restrained.

THE FIRST DAY THE HAMSTER JUMPED A LOT
BUT KEPT HITTING THE TRANSPARENT COVER.
THE NEXT DAY IT JUMPED A BIT LESS.

After a few days the hamster gave up entirely. Researchers then removed the cover, but the hamster never tried to jump out again. After failing a few times, it became convinced that it had no chance of success. Even though the conditions had changed, the hamster was still convinced about the inescapability of its situation. The state this hamster was in is known as **learned helplessness**, and it is something we too can encounter.

Unhappiness and the feeling that "I can't do it" are typical for being in a state of helplessness. To help better illustrate the point, we are going to refer to being in this state as having a "**hamster**." Thus, when we write that someone "**has a hamster**" or that they have "**caught a hamster**," it should be clear what situation they are in. If you want to be happier in life, you need to learn how to spot the hamsters and get rid of them.

Another example of learned helplessness can also be observed on elephant farms. (This time I am talking about real elephants.) These enormous animals are usually tied in place with a very thin rope. If an elephant wanted to, it could easily break free.

But imagine that this elephant had been tied up with the same rope since it was a baby. The baby animal tried to free itself, but was unable to break the rope. After failing a few times it became convinced that escape is impossible. The elephant started to believe in its inability that it gave up trying. Even as it has grown in size and strength, it still believes that the rope can't be broken. To use our terminology: "The elephant has caught a hamster."

AFTER SEVERAL DAYS, THE COVER WAS REMOVED.
THE HAMSTER, HOWEVER, NEVER TRIED TO ESCAPE.
IT FELL INTO A STATE OF LEARNED HELPLESSNESS.

WHEN IT WAS SMALL, THE ELEPHANT BECAME CONVINCED THAT IT WOULD NEVER BREAK THE ROPE. WHEN IT GREW UP, IT NEVER EVEN TRIED.

Some of the causes of procrastination can be traced to the hamster. Spending your time doing nothing will often make you feel guilty. Guilt will make you doubt yourself. Doubts will lower your self-confidence and will lead to feeling helpless. In the end, as a result of this you end up doing nothing. The cycle repeats itself. You have caught a "procrastination hamster."

Being stuck with a hamster and in a state of depression in the long term isn't helpful; it's a state no one would probably choose to be in voluntarily. Thus, from time to time you should ask yourself if the imaginary cover on your box is open and if it isn't time to try jumping out again.

How do you know when you have a hamster?

You are apathetic and don't feel like doing anything. You lack energy, and your cognitive resources are depleted. You don't believe in yourself and see everything in a negative light. You doubt even things that you

THE PROCRASTINATION HAMSTER LOOP:

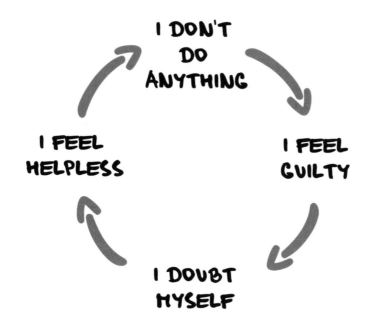

believed in relatively recently. You view your situation as being without hope. You tend to procrastinate a lot. Sometimes you even want to give in to the hamster and pity yourself.

If you are experiencing this mix of unpleasant feelings, it is time you gave a name to your problem and admitted it: "Yes. I have a hamster." Giving a name to your problems is the first step to getting out of them.

How Can You Fight Your Hamster? Like a Veteran

If you want to know how to overcome a hamster, inspiration can be found in a group of American veterans. Depression and even suicide rates were high among these people. Therapists from the Hawaii Psychological Association were nonetheless able to find a way to help them.[83] You can use the same method they developed to overcome your hamster.

Philip Zimbardo's studies have shown that the human brain works in different *time perspectives*.[84] These determine how much time you spend thinking about the future, the present, and the negative and positive aspects of the past. People can be divided into being *future-oriented*, *present-oriented*, *past-negative-oriented*, and *past-positive-oriented*.

What kind of time perspective did the veterans have? Due to their wartime experiences, they were largely focused on the negative past. Most of them were convinced that they were nearing the end of their lives, and therefore they had hardly any orientation towards the future.

OUR BRAINS WORK IN FOUR DIFFERENT TIME PERSPECTIVES:
PAST-POSITIVE-ORIENTED, PAST-NEGATIVE-ORIENTED,
PRESENT-ORIENTED, **AND** FUTURE-ORIENTED.

People in this frame of mind will easily catch a hamster. Since they focus very little on positive things in the past, they don't believe in themselves and because they are too little future-oriented they lack intrinsic motivation. Their brains waste energy doubting and thinking about negative experiences from the past. This elicits unpleasant feelings, which generate new bad memories, which serve only to strengthen their past-negative orientation. It is one long downward hamster spiral.

How were the researchers able to help the veterans with their depression?

The first step was to help them **increase their future-orientation**. The researchers reminded them of the value of time and asked them what they would like to devote theirs to. This helped spark the flame of their personal vision: the light at the end of the helplessness tunnel. Several veterans decided they would write their memoirs while others found meaning in giving lectures to young people.

But just increasing intrinsic motivation and becoming more future-oriented is not enough. If these newly motivated veterans failed, they would just be adding another negative experience to their life and essentially feeding their hamster. Therefore, it was necessary to help them **cope with their negative past** and teach them to **switch their orientation from past-negative to the past-positive**.

So, what was the next step? The researchers steered the veterans towards realizing that although what they had experienced was horrible, it would enable them to bear witness to war, which might help lower the chances of wars developing in the future. The researchers helped them view the worst things they had experienced from a more positive perspective.

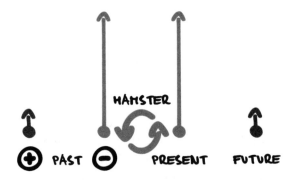

PEOPLE WHO ARE LOW ON FUTURE AND PAST-POSITIVE ORIENTATION AND AT THE SAME TIME HIGH ON PRESENT AND PAST-NEGATIVE ORIENTATION GET HAMSTERS MORE OFTEN.

If you manage to increase your orientation towards the future and at the same time can switch from viewing negatives as positives, the result is something that we have already discussed in the chapter about motivation. A feedback loop is created that is the total opposite of a hamster. The **state of flow** will emerge.

How can you become more future-oriented? The key lies in working with **intrinsic motivation** and reminding yourself of your **Personal vision**. If you think more about the future, you will train your brain to imagine it more vividly.

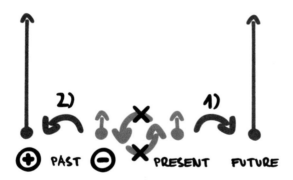

YOU CAN GET OUT OF THE HAMSTER LOOP BY:
1) BECOMING MORE FUTURE-ORIENTED.
2) TURNING A PAST-NEGATIVE ORIENTATION INTO A POSITIVE ONE.

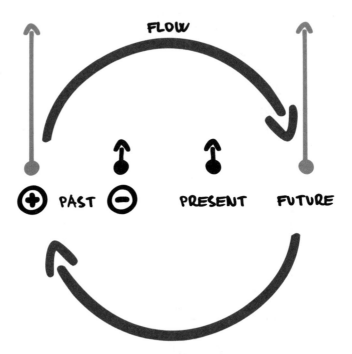

IN BETWEEN ORIENTATION TOWARDS THE FUTURE AND THE PAST-POSITIVE ARISES THE FLOW FEEDBACK LOOP.

THE POSITIVE FLOW LOOP:

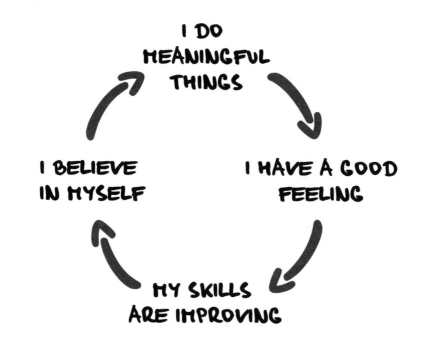

How can you change the manner in which you view your past? How can you better deal with failure? How can you learn to treat negative things more positively? Our method for turning negative things into positive ones is called the **Inner-switch** method.

TOOL: Inner-Switch

Before Viktor Frankl became one of the most well-known psychiatrists of the second half of the twentieth century, he had an extremely difficult life. Due to his Jewish descent, he was deported to the Auschwitz concentration camp. He was one of the few to survive the horrors of this place. What he lived through would later go on to significantly impact his career in therapy.

In his writings, Frankl describes how even in concentration camps there were people who managed not to lose hope and to remain emotionally balanced.[85] Based on these experiences, he later became a pioneer of the idea that people have **a free response to surrounding stimuli**. It describes that between a stimulus and the response to it there is a space

THE FREEDOM TO CHOOSE A RESPONSE:

STIMULUS   RESPONSE

FREEDOM

in which we can consciously choose how the stimuli will affect us. This concept became the base of the Inner-switch skill.

Your **Inner-switch** will help you consciously switch negative stimuli into neutral or even positive ones. If you learn how to play this inner game, negative stimuli will no longer automatically elicit negative emotional responses. Despite the fact that you are unable to influence many events in life, by flipping your Inner-switch you can choose how they affect you.

STANDARD RESPONSE:

STIMULUS   RESPONSE

AUTOMATICALLY

INNER SWITCH:

STIMULUS   RESPONSE

INNER-SWITCH

BY FLIPPING YOUR INNER-SWITCH YOU CAN LEARN
TO RESPOND TO NEGATIVE STIMULI IN A NEUTRAL
WAY OR EVEN IN A POSITIVE ONE.

Just like Heroism, your Inner-switch is also a **micro-habit**. It should always be on your mind and it is a skill that you can improve through training.

There are three ways to use this method: first it is **changing how you view your failures**, then **overcoming the blows of fate**, and finally **turning a negative past into a positive one**.

Managing Your Failures

Thomas J. Watson, the former CEO of IBM, once stated: *"If you want to succeed, double your failure rate."* Many people, however, view their failures as something bad. Failure elicits negative emotions that lower their self-confidence and induce feelings of helplessness. This can lead to catching a hamster.

Imagine a smoker that is trying to quit. He makes it ten days without a cigarette but then fails and lights one up. Instead of feeling good about himself for managing to be cigarette-free for ten days and knowing that next time he will do better, negative thoughts and doubts overwhelm him. He starts to think he doesn't have what it takes to succeed and that maybe he will never quit smoking. A hamster is born.

Here is another example. Imagine a young man who meets the girl of his dreams on a bus. He looks at her the entire trip, works up the courage to talk to her, and finally as he gets off he says, "Hi, could I have your number?" She responds, frowning with a hint of disgust: "No." If this young man only views this experience as negative he will begin to doubt himself, which increases his chances of failure in the future.

Imagine if a month later that same young man finds himself in a similar situation: a different bus, a different girl. Once again he makes another attempt at talking to the girl, his voice now even more nervous. And he is rejected once again. These few failures have convinced him that he will never be successful; perhaps he will never even try to approach a girl again. He could catch a dating hamster.

Why do people view failure as something bad? How can you learn to not have negative feelings about it? How can you avoid the hamsters of failure?

The culture we have grown up in teaches us that failure is bad. When a small child touches the stove and burns his hand, his parents will most likely yell at him. Or when a student gets a bad grade he will most probably experience social pressure and become the joke of the class. Some people even view those who fail as if something bad has happened to them (and hence the shameful label of "loser" was born).

It is critical to learn how to take the opposite view of failure. Failure can be viewed as a necessary ingredient in the recipe for future success. But aren't these just empty phrases? Why do we need failure?

First of all, whenever you fail to succeed at something, you enter the *learning zone*.[86] In this state your brain is capable of learning new things that you would otherwise never learn. Thanks to this, your chances of managing a similar situation in the future are increased.

Second of all, in spite of failure, just trying was already beneficial. It means you have left your comfort zone and have performed an act of small heroism. As my grandfather used to say, *"Even falling flat on your face is a step forward."*

That's why it pays to come to grips with the fact that failure is and will be a part of every journey towards fulfilling a personal vision. You need to learn to overcome failure, to avoid negative feelings, and ideally to look forward to failure from time to time. You learn new skills in the learning zone. It is important to always do the best you can and not think so much about the results.

FAILURE   REACTION

⊖ ⌇⌇⌇⌇⌇⟶ ⠺ / ☺

INNER-SWITCH

IN ORDER TO DEAL WITH FAILURE, IT IS GOOD TO REALIZE:
1) YOU CAN FLIP YOUR INNER-SWITCH. YOU HAVE THE FREEDOM TO CHOOSE.
2) FAILURE PUTS YOU IN THE LEARNING ZONE.
3) YOU HAVE TRIED TO MOVE FORWARD - HEROISM.
4) RESULTS DON'T MATTER, PUTTING IN MAXIMUM EFFORT DOES.

Our smoker should feel good that he stayed smoke-free for an entire ten days with the knowledge that next time he will hold on for at least eleven days. The young man from the bus should be proud of himself for trying and should believe that the experience he has gained will help him to meet a girl next time.

Failure allows you to flip your **Inner-switch**. Remember, it is up to you alone what feelings failure causes. You have the freedom to choose your response. When you fail, it's a good idea to tell yourself: "Now, I have freedom. I can flip my Inner-switch. I can choose how this failure will affect me." The more often you remind yourself of your Inner-switch, the better you will handle failure.

Overcoming the Blows of Fate

There is a certain likelihood that at some point or another fate will un-expectedly drop a brick on your head. If this ever happens to you, you need to use your Inner-switch in a different mode, in one based on the idea that *"Success doesn't mean you never fall; it means you know how to get up quick."*

Very unpleasant experiences can elicit depression and what is called **post-traumatic stress syndrome** (or to put it in our terminology: "an ul-tra-hamster"). For some people though, personal tragedy can become an impulse that drives them forward in life. This is known as **post-traumat-ic growth**.[87] Whether you succumb to post-traumatic stress or you ex-perience post-traumatic growth is once again all up to you—it's a higher

WHEN FATE DROPS A BRICK ON YOUR HEAD, YOU NEED TO LEARN HOW TO WIN YOUR INNER-SWITCH AND GET UP AS QUICKLY AS POSSIBLE.

level of ability to use your Inner-switch. Whether you succumb to stress or you experience growth is once again all up to you—it's all about playing your inner game at a higher level.

When a blow of fate leaves you with a hamster, you should get rid of it as quickly as possible. The quicker you can dust yourself off and stand up, the sooner you will be able to get back to living life to its fullest.

Randy Pausch has greatly inspired me. This American professor found out that he had terminal cancer; the doctors told him he had only about six months to live. Instead of becoming depressed, Randy began living the half year of life he had left to the fullest. He gave a talk he titled "The Last Lecture" in which he summarized his life (millions of people have since watched it on the Internet), he wrote a book, and spent the rest of his time with his family.[88]

The story of Randy Pausch reminds me that most of the problems we face in life aren't real problems. His approach to life has shown me that even when fate dumps the biggest brick ever on your head, it doesn't mean you need to resign from life.

It is most likely that at some point or another in life, fate will deliver you a blow or two. To get yourself prepared for them, you should practice using your Inner-switch to overcome less serious obstacles. Through training you can increase the chances of being at least a little bit prepared if something serious happens to you. As Randy Pausch expressed: *"The brick walls are there to stop the other people."*

Switching from the Negative Past to the Positive One

It is hard to evaluate if past events were "good" or "bad." Everything we have experienced in life is from a certain perspective important; our experiences form our personalities and have made us who we are today. When we look back on something and say that it was bad, this is often only a reflection of our attitude towards it. Our attitudes towards past events however can be changed by flipping our **Inner-switch**. Doing so can help us discover the positive things about the past. Recall the veterans and how they coped with the horrors of war. Frankl himself put it this way: *"Man is ready and willing to shoulder any suffering as soon and as long as he can see a meaning in it."*

One of my clients moved away from home at a very young age to escape the poor relationships in her family. Whenever she thought about it, she would quickly catch a hamster. During one of our meetings, I asked her how this event moved her forward and what could be seen as beneficial about it.

She slowly came to realize that maybe thanks to her independence she had started her own business and had become interested in interpersonal relationships as well as her own development. In the end, she came to the conclusion that the event she had once considered to be the worst in her life provided her with an essential learning experience. Once she processed her past, she was able to change her attitude towards it and break the hamster cycle.

There are two types of hamsters. The first kind can be dealt with; the second kind you can't do anything about.

Imagine that you are deep in a thicket of thorn bushes. Some of the thorns can be broken off so that they no longer prick you. Others are too strong to be broken. These ones however can be dulled so they don't prick you but just push you. Just as the tips of some thorns can be broken off while others can just be dulled, some hamsters can be dealt with while others you just need to cope with as quickly as possible.

How can you pacify your hamsters? How can you dull thorns? Take a piece of paper and try out the following additional method we call the *Hamster analysis*.

It's not the best idea to deal with all of your problems at once. That's why it's worth it to work on your hamsters gradually. Work on one at a time. Ask yourself how you have benefited from each hamster and how it has moved you forward. Write it down. Once you have "dulled" one hamster, you can come back to your sheet in about a week or so before dealing with another hamster.

Just like for learning new habits, you should also use the **kaizen** method here: by taking small steps you can make big changes that last.

THORNS:

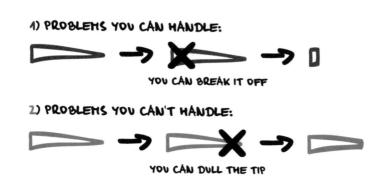

1) PROBLEMS YOU CAN HANDLE:

YOU CAN BREAK IT OFF

2) PROBLEMS YOU CAN'T HANDLE:

YOU CAN DULL THE TIP

PROBLEMS YOU CAN DO SOMETHING ABOUT SHOULD BE DEALT WITH AS SOON AS POSSIBLE - BREAK OFF THE THORN.
PROBLEMS YOU CAN'T DO ANYTHING ABOUT SHOULD BE WEAKENED UNTIL THEY NO LONGER AFFECT YOU - DULL THE THORNS.

HAMSTER ANALYSIS:

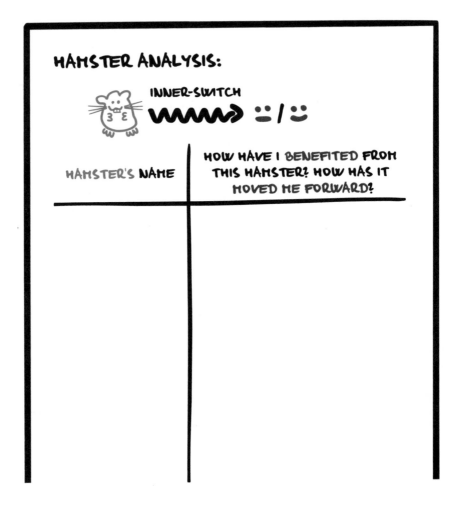

INNER-SWITCH

HAMSTER'S NAME	HOW HAVE I BENEFITED FROM THIS HAMSTER? HOW HAS IT MOVED ME FORWARD?

Once you start using a Hamster analysis, you will find that the hamsters from your past will gradually cease to affect you negatively.

In the following chapter we will describe the **Flow-list**, which will enable you to become more past-positive-oriented, help you avoid new hamsters, and gain greater emotional stability.

TOOL: Flow-List

Martin Seligman has dealt with the high rate of suicide and depression in the US Army. His extensive study on half a million soldiers revealed a group of methods that can help people achieve long-lasting happiness.[89] After half a year of using them, suicide and depression rates had been reduced significantly. So what was the key?

Our tool, which we have call the **Flow-list**, draws from Seligman's research. It is based on daily writing down **three positive things** that have happened to you. Then next to those things, rate on a scale of 1 to 10 how happy you were that day (1-very little happiness, 10-the greatest happiness imaginable, 5-average). This simple tool will help you systematically become more past-positive-oriented, which will help overcome not only your hamsters and depression, but it will also have long term effects on your happiness.

The Flow-list, similar to the Habit-list, should be filled in with care every day. This method will only take a few minutes, but after only a month you will evaluate your life as being much happier.[90]

How exactly do you use this tool? Take a seat every evening and write down the three most positive things that happened in your day. If you don't have big things, it doesn't matter. Write down small things or thing you are grateful for. Try to describe these things in a few sentences so that later you will be able to recall them, just as you take pictures on vacation to remind you what you have experienced.

Sometimes three positive experiences might not come to you immediately. No worries. It is part of the process. Keep thinking. By doing so your brain will learn how to switch from being past-negative-oriented to past-positive.

Daniel Kahneman's research has shown that people have a tendency to judge their entire life based on their current mood.[91] When they are feeling good, they will deem the entire past to be positive as well. In contrast, when people are unhappy in the present, they have a tendency to view their entire life in a negative light.

The Flow-list will help you avoid this phenomenon. You can go through your Flow-list whenever you want. This gives you clear feedback—the truth about your former happiness. This will also help you recall pleasant past experiences, which will contribute to improving your current mood.

We have created a Flow-list template for you, which you can download here: **www.procrastination.com/flow-list**. You can even add the habit of filling in your Flow-list to one of the columns in your Habit-list.

FLOW-LIST:

	I	II	III	🙂 1..10
1.				
2.				
3.				
⋮				

THE FLOW-LIST COVERS ONE MONTH. EACH ROW EQUALS ONE DAY AND THE COLUMNS CONTAIN ONE OF THE THREE POSITIVE THINGS THAT HAPPENED TO YOU THAT DAY. IN THE LAST COLUMN YOU RATE HOW HAPPY YOU WERE ON A SCALE OF 1 TO 10.

TOOL: Hamster-Restart

It is only a matter of time before a **hamster** pops up in your life. Being in a bad mood here and there isn't a bad thing. It will give you a comparison and make you appreciate more the days when you are happy. However, being stuck with a hamster for days on end is not a good thing at all, and therefore you need to learn how to get rid of it as fast as possible. We call this method *Hamster-restart*:

- First of all you need to **recognize** the situation you are in and give it a **name**: "Yes. I have a hamster."

- In order to fight against your hamster, **replenish your cognitive resources**. Do some exercise, drink a glass of fresh juice, have some fruit, or take a five-minute walk. If you really feel like you don't have any energy, go and have a guilt-free nap.

- Get to know your enemy. **Remind yourself how the hamster works.** When a hamster has taken over, it is normal that everything seems meaningless, and that you are full of doubt, feel powerless, and are overall in a negative mood.

- **Come to the realization that you have to start with yourself.** Whether you get rid of your hamster or not depends mostly on you. It's not good to rationalize and blame the world around you. As John Whitmore wrote in his book: *"We all like to believe that the problem is with other people. It gives us the feeling that our actions are right and that we can't change anything ourselves."* The truth is that you are often the one who is responsible for your happiness or unhappiness.

- Turn negatives into positives. **Use your Inner-switch.**
- **Become more future-oriented.** Don't forget about the value of time and your Personal vision. Remind yourself why it is not rational to be stuck with a hamster and why you want to live your life to the fullest.
- **Become more past-positive-oriented.** Hamsters like wallowing in negativity. They have blinders on their eyes that block out positive information. Remind yourself of it. Go over your list of personal achievements as well as your Flow-list.
- **Break the hamster cycle.** Press the imaginary red "Hamster-restart button." Close the door on your bad mood. Remember this quotation: *"Success doesn't mean you never fall; it means you know how to get up quick."*
- **Prepare your new To-Do today** and plan out the tasks you will do. Include activities that will help you achieve the state of flow.
- **Practice Heroism**, leave your comfort zone and move forward. Begin to work on your To-Do today tasks. You'll find that in just a few minutes your hamster will disappear.

HAMSTER RESTART:
INSTRUCTIONS FOR USE

1) REALIZE THAT YOU HAVE A HAMSTER
2) TAKE A REST AND REPLENISH YOUR COGNITIVE RESOURCES
3) REMIND YOURSELF OF THE THEORY HOW THE HAMSTER WORKS
4) REALIZE THAT IT IS MOSTLY UP TO YOU IF YOU GET RID OF YOUR HAMSTER
5) FLIP YOUR INNER SWITCH; TURN NEGATIVES INTO POSITIVES
6) BECOME MORE FUTURE-ORIENTED: REMIND YOURSELF OF YOUR VISION AND THE VALUE OF TIME
7) BECOME MORE PAST-POSITIVE-ORIENTED: GO OVER YOUR FLOW SHEET AND YOUR LIST OF PERSONAL ACHIEVEMENTS
8) PRESS THE HAMSTER RESTART BUTTON AND START ANEW AND BETTER
9) PREPARE YOUR TO-DO-TODAY
10) PRACTICE HEROISM AND START WORKING ON YOUR FIRST TASK

HAMSTER
RESTART

Personal Growth and Personal Decline

Life doesn't change gradually, but often it changes in leaps and bounds. It is influenced by two **feedback loops**.

First, there is the **positive flow loop**. The more successful you are, the happier you will be, and thus the more you will believe in yourself and your personal vision. More dopamine will make you more creative and help you learn more effectively. You will end up being even more successful.

On the other hand, there is the **negative hamster loop**. You fail, stop believing in yourself, and doubt yourself and the meaning of life. Because of a low dopamine level you aren't creative, are incapable of learning well, have low self-confidence, and suffer from paralysis and procrastination.

Many people fluctuate between these two loops without being drawn into either. It is only once you cross the **tipping point** that one of these loops is activated.

The purpose of this book is to give people the tools they need to help create and maintain a positive flow loop. Therefore, all of these tools are ingeniously interlinked:

1. A **Personal vision** will increase your intrinsic motivation, make you more future-oriented, and remind you of the value of time.
2. A **Habit-list** will strengthen your cognitive resources and tame your elephant.

3. The **To-Do today** will help you keep your tasks in order and plan your time better.
4. **Heroism** will teach you to leave your comfort zone.
5. A **Flow-list** will make you more past-positive-oriented.
6. Your **Inner-switch** will help you turn negatives into positives.
7. The **Hamster-restart** will get you back on track if you get thrown significantly off course.

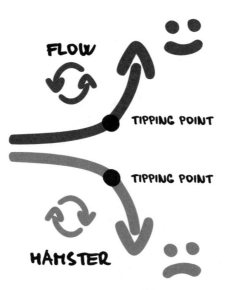

PERSONAL GROWTH AND PERSONAL DECLINE DON'T
HAPPEN GRADUALLY. ONCE YOU GO BEYOND THE TIPPING
POINT, YOU ENTER ONE OF TWO FEEDBACK LOOPS: EITHER
THE FLOW LOOP IN THE CASE OF GROWTH OR THE HAMSTER
LOOP IN THE CASE OF DECLINE.

Chapter Recap: Outcomes

If you fulfill your vision through doing the right actions, you will receive **emotional and material outcomes**. You will be happy and able to see the results of your work.

Even though you may be fulfilling your vision, sometimes something will throw you off track causing you to lose happiness. Being in a bad mood occasionally isn't such a horrible thing, but you do need to know how to quickly get out of it.

The part of your brain known as the **amygdala** is constantly looking for danger in all that we perceive and magnifies **negative stimuli**. If there are many, the amygdala will notice mainly them and will stop noticing the positive ones. This will make you unhappy.

Unhappiness and negative emotions are **socially contagious** and may result in collective pessimism in which people reinforce each other.

A few failures or negative stimuli might induce a state of **learned helplessness**—you can catch a **hamster**.

You can get rid of hamsters by becoming more **future-oriented** and at the same time by switching from being past-negative to being **past-positive-oriented**. The tools of the Inner-switch and Flow-list will help you with this.

The micro-habit of flipping your **Inner-switch** is based on your freedom to choose how the outside world influences you. You can use this method to overcome your failures, to handle the blows of fate, and to cope with negative past experiences.

The **Flow-list** is a tool that is based on the idea that if you write down three positive things that happened to you every day, you can become happier and more past-positive-oriented.

The **Hamster-restart** is a one-off tool that can get you back on track once you have been thrown off course and have found yourself in a state of learned helplessness.

A **hamster** feedback loop as well as a **flow** feedback loop exist, both of which influence your motivation, discipline, and thus your outcomes. Where hamsters can be found, there is fertile ground for procrastination. In contrast, the more you are in your flow, the less you will procrastinate.

How happy were you last month in average? How would you assess the real outcomes of your work? Now, once again on a scale of 1 to 10, rate your emotional and material **outcomes** and how well you are using the methods described in this chapter.

Just as I have done in the other chapters, here I recommend that you re-evaluate yourself in the future and update your self-assessment. You will see that as you use these tools and your ratings increase, your overall outcomes will improve. I hope this chapter will make you happier and more balanced. Once you have learned how to improve your **motivation**, **discipline**, and **outcomes**, there is only one piece of the personal development puzzle missing: **objectivity.***

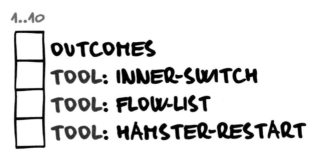

1..10

OUTCOMES
TOOL: INNER-SWITCH
TOOL: FLOW-LIST
TOOL: HAMSTER-RESTART

---

*   *Author's note:* I consider objectivity to be the most important subject of all. Of the four major topics covered in this book, this one has the deepest meaning for me, which perhaps at first glance might not be so easy to grasp. In my experience, however, objectivity has the potential to move you forward the most in life.

OBJECTIVITY

LEARNING HOW TO SEE YOUR FLAWS

McArthur Wheeler of Pittsburgh robbed two banks in broad daylight without any attempt at disguising himself. When security camera footage broadcast on the news led to his identification and the police arrested him shortly afterwards, he was thoroughly shocked at having been recognized. After being caught, he stared in disbelief and mumbled: "But I wore the juice!"[92]

We humans perceive the world around us with our senses (since you are able to read this book right now, this goes for you, too). Everything that we see, hear, or otherwise sense, travels to our brains as a stream of data without meaning. Our brains assess the data and based on them we make decisions. These decisions then determine our subsequent actions and resulting behavior.

If the heat receptors in your mouth tell you that you are drinking boiling hot tea, you spit it out. If you have the feeling that someone has done you wrong, you protect yourself. When you are driving and all of a sudden you see the red lights of the car in front of you, you immediately react by moving your foot from the gas pedal and you begin to brake.

The rules your brain follows to make decisions are called *mental models*. These models are ideas stored in our brains about how the world around us works.[93]

Each of our mental models can be assessed for how well it corresponds to reality. We call this level **objectivity**. Thinking that banging your head against the ground will solve famine in Africa would most likely be very low on the objectivity scale. On the contrary, a mental

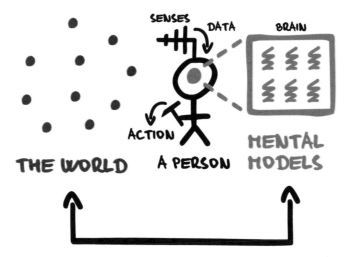

PEOPLE PERCEIVE THE OUTSIDE WORLD WITH THEIR SENSES.
THE DATA SENSES TRAVEL TO THE BRAIN, THE BRAIN THEN
USES MENTAL MODELS TO EVALUATE THEM AND MAKE DECISIONS.
THESE DECISIONS THEN INFLUENCE SUBSEQUENT ACTIONS AND
RESULTING BEHAVIOR. MENTAL MODELS ARE STORED IDEAS IN
OUR BRAINS ABOUT HOW THE OUTSIDE WORLD WORKS.

LEVEL OF OBJECTIVITY:

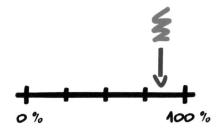

MENTAL MODELS CAN BE ASSIGNED A PROBABILITY OF HOW WELL THEY CORRESPOND TO REALITY.

model that describes that if you shoot yourself in the head it will kill you indicates a relatively high level of objectivity.

The problem with the human brain is that it tends to succumb to what is known as the *Dunning-Kruger effect*.[94] In our heads, we have mental models that we firmly believe in, even though they do not correspond to reality. People often confuse their subjective notions with objective facts.

Recent research has demonstrated that some of our subjective notions of how the world works elicit the same types of feelings as do ob-

NONOBJECTIVITY:

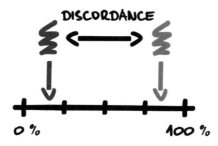

PEOPLE OFTEN SUBJECTIVELY ASCRIBE A DEGREE OF PROBABILITY TO THEIR MENTAL MODELS THAT DO NOT CORRESPOND TO THE OBJECTIVE ONE. THEY OFTEN BELIEVE IN THINGS THAT ARE NOT TRUE.

jective facts such as "2 + 2 = 4."[95] We feel totally certain that they are absolutely true. However, our brains are relatively often wrong about this feeling of absolute surety.

The thief Wheeler thought that if he covered his face (and even his eyes) in lemon juice, he would be invisible to video cameras. He believed this so much that he fearlessly went and robbed two banks covered in juice. To us a senseless model was for him the irrefutable truth. Wheeler attributed absolute subjective certainty to his nonobjective model. He was suffering from the Dunning-Kruger effect.

The Dunning-Kruger Effect and the Blindness of the Incompetent

Wheeler's lemon juice story inspired researchers David Dunning and Justin Kruger to study this phenomenon in greater detail. The researchers were intrigued by the obvious difference in people's actual abilities and how they perceive these abilities. Dunning and Kruger hypothesized that incompetent people suffer from two types of problems:

- Due to their incompetence, they **make flawed decisions** (such as robbing a bank while covered in lemon juice).
- They **are unable to realize** the fact that they make flawed decisions. (Not even the video footage convinced Wheeler of his inability to be invisible; he claimed that it was faked.)

The researchers tested the validity of these hypotheses on a sample of participants. First they filled out a test measuring their abilities in a certain domain (logical reasoning, grammar, and humor). Then, the participants were asked to assess how good their abilities were. The researchers discovered two interesting findings:

- *The least competent people* (labeled *incompetent* in the research) had a tendency to significantly **overestimate their abilities**. In fact, the less competent they were, the more they overestimated themselves. For example, the more painfully unfunny an individual was, the funnier they thought they were. This effect was elegantly described by Charles Darwin years ago: *"Ignorance more frequently begets con-*

fidence than does knowledge."

- The second interesting finding was that the most competent participants had a tendency to **underestimate their abilities**. Their underrated results can be explained by the fact that if a task seems easy to them, they will have the feeling that the task is easy even for other people.

In another part of the experiment, participants had the possibility to review the test results of other people. They were subsequently asked to conduct a self-assessment again.

Competent participants realized that they were better off than they had thought. Thus, they modified their self-assessments and began to evaluate themselves more objectively.

Once **incompetent** participants were confronted with reality, however, they didn't change their nonobjective self-assessments. They were unable to recognize that the abilities of others were better than theirs. In the words of Forrest Gump: *"Stupid is, as stupid does."*

In short, this **study found** that people who don't know, don't know that they don't know. Incompetent people have a tendency to significantly overestimate their own abilities; they are unable to assess the abilities of others, and not even after being confronted with reality do they change their perception of themselves. In this book, when we talk about people with this problem, we will simply say that they "have a case of Dunning-Kruger" (or DK for short). This research demonstrates that when people come to nonobjective and false conclusions, it is their non-objectivity that prevents them from recognizing and admitting it.

THE DUNNING-KRUGER EFFECT:

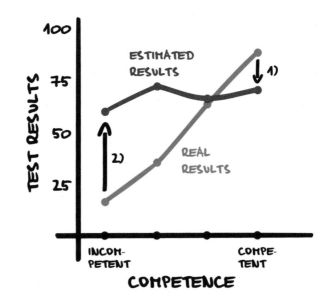

THE RESEARCH SHOWED TWO MAIN THINGS:
1) COMPETENT PEOPLE HAVE A TENDENCY TO UNDERESTIMATE THEMSELVES
2) INCOMPETENT PEOPLE HAVE A TENDENCY TO OVERESTIMATE THEMSELVES

Sweet Ignorance: The Guardian of Our Brain

The medical condition known as *anosognosia* indicates that the Dunning-Kruger effect may be a protective mechanism built into the human brain. It is a type of brain damage that can be found in people who have lost a limb. People suffering from anosognosia think they still have the limb, and they cannot be convinced otherwise.[96]

When a doctor speaks with such a patient about his or her healthy left hand, the patient communicates normally. When the conversation turns to the missing right hand, the patient is pretending not to hear what the doctor is saying. Brain scans have shown that this is not a conscious response; instead, the patient's damaged brain subconsciously blocks information about his or her missing limb.[97]

There have even been cases in which blind people were unable to be convinced that they were blind.[98] Such extreme examples of anosognosia support the theory that our brains are able to ignore information pointing to our incompetence.

For the brain of the lemon juice bandit, it was simpler to say the evidence was faked than to admit his own incompetence and nonobjectivity.

Similar to with anosognosia, the human brain often responds to information demonstrating that our mental models are false simply by ignoring it. Thus, our brains keep us in a state of nonobjectivity and sweet ignorance. But is nonobjectivity always so sweet? What are the risks involved? Why should we bother to be objective?

Why Fight Nonobjectivity?

Once I had a classmate who wasn't particularly funny. To put it precisely, many people considered him to be really awkward. Whenever he told a joke, lots of people really laughed. Unfortunately, they weren't laughing with him, but at him. My classmate most likely interpreted this laughter as a confirmation of his sense of humor. Thus, he kept telling more and more jokes.

Even though many years have since passed, it wouldn't surprise me if he still behaves the same way today. Would you like to be like him? Would you like to go through life with everyone seeing your flaws, your Dunning-Kruger, except for you? Why is it important to strive for your own objectivity?

- **More objective mental models result in more frequent better decisions.** Better models help you predict the consequences of your behavior more accurately. In contrast, if you have nonobjective models and are suffering from Dunning-Kruger, your actions will not have the consequences you intended. Exaggerated self-confidence is no guarantee of success. Lemon juice will simply not make you invisible.
- **Nonobjectivity prevents personal growth.** Sometimes, I encounter managers who are convinced that they are the best leaders in the world. Unfortunately, they are often the only ones in their failing companies who think so. Another reason to increase your objectivity is that you can only begin working on your flaws once you

recognize them. Therefore, looking for your own Dunning-Krugers is probably one of the most important things you can do for your personal development.

- **Nonobjectivity, even with good intentions, can harm others.** There is a reason they say: *"The road to hell is paved with good intentions."* The third and main reason why you should fight nonobjectivity was expressed once again by Bertrand Russell when he said: *"Men have caused the most suffering to other men because they were convinced about things that turned out to be untrue."*

For example, many mass murderers, long after they have committed their horrible crimes, still think they did the right thing and have never considered themselves to be bad people. Just take a look at how Anders Breivik presented himself at his trial. He was firmly convinced that he had done the right thing. His mental models hadn't changed.

How can you fight against your own nonobjectivity? How can you avoid the Dunning-Kruger effect? How can you find your flaws and increase your objectivity in the long term?

How Exactly Can You Increase Objectivity?

Objectivity and truth are one of the most important values for society to function and grow. The Dunning-Kruger effect is their enemy. It is particularly treacherous because it can block out objectivity directly in our heads. Don't let yourself fall into this trap. The following principles will help you fight against the Dunning-Kruger effect and nonobjectivity.

- **Increase your competence through education** – In another experiment, Dunning and Kruger discovered that training and education can help incompetent people assess themselves and others more accurately.[99] If you improve your abilities in a certain area, you will be able to recognize how incompetent you used to be. Socrates expressed the importance of education when he said, *"The only good is knowledge and the only evil is ignorance."*

- **Build your foundation on good sources of information** – Judging the quality of sources in today's information age is critical. Today anyone can put any information on the Internet with ease; therefore, you need to learn how to assess the quality of what is available. You can expect that knowledge contained in academic journals and research studies is more reliable than information from the tabloids or from anonymous blogs. If the facts in the text have references to the sources that they are based on, it indicates that the author has tried to be more objective. Wikipedia, for example, encourages its contributors to include lists of sources referenced for every article. It is not possible for the human brain to understand in precise detail all of the laws of how the world works. Therefore, every mental model is just a simplification and is thus always partially inaccurate. But as Bertrand Russell once said: *"When one admits that nothing is certain one must, I think, also admit that some things are much more nearly certain than others."*

- **Do not have strong views on things you know little about** – A lack of information or information skewed by the media are fertile ground for the Dunning-Kruger effect. Just look at the comments sections on news sites. You will find posters who think they are experts on everything. If you want to avoid nonobjectivity, share your opinion about things that you are truly competent in. Don't transfer competence in one field to another. Just because someone is a successful zoologist doesn't mean they understand graphic design. You don't have to have an opinion about everything. It is better to admit that you don't know or that you don't have an opinion. Richard Feynman, who won the Nobel Prize in physics, once declared: *"I think it's much more interesting to live not knowing than to have answers which might be wrong."*

- **Question your intuition** – Don't just doubt, actively question. Doubt itself won't get you anywhere. However, if you are constantly calling things into question, you are actively looking for imperfections in your mental models and ways to improve them. As behavioral economist Dan Ariely's research has demonstrated, our intuition is often wrong.[100] This is what he has to say about the matter: *"We—and by* *that I mean You, Me, Companies, and Policy Makers—need to doubt our intuitions. If we keep following gut and common wisdom or doing what is easiest or most habitual just because, 'well, things have always been done that way,' we will continue to make mistakes."* Be an everyday hero by questioning your own opinions. Actively looking for things that you are wrong about is one of the biggest discomfort zones.

- **Search out external feedback** – Start actively questioning your subjective opinions. Collect the opinions of those around you. After each of my workshops, I ask the participants for their anonymous feedback and assessment. On several occasions I have felt that a particular workshop was one of the very best I had ever held, but the participants' feedback indicated that it had been just average. Other times I have thought it was bad, but the evaluations I received indicated the total opposite. These experiences have confirmed my impression that sometimes it is better to trust external feedback more than your own subjective opinion. Even if at first you don't agree with the feedback you get, always try to take something from it. Don't just turn a blind eye.

- **Work on your critical thinking skills** – This style of thinking entails the freedom to think for yourself and to not uncritically accept the ideas of authority figures and others. It also indicates to you if certain information is true or not. If it leads you to a different opinion than everyone else, have the courage to share it. Bertrand Russell described the heroism it takes to leave your comfort zone and express your opinion in the following manner: *"To save the world requires faith and courage: faith in reason, and courage to proclaim what reason shows to be true."*

- **Try to refute your ideas just as intensely as you try to confirm them** – Not long ago an acquaintance boasted to me that he regularly "stares at the sun at high noon" for several minutes at a time. He claims it improves his vision. In addition, he also explained to me how pharmaceutical companies have kept this "miraculous" method hushed up so that they can get rich off of selling their medicine. When you search the Internet, you can find information that verifies almost any claim: even the idea that staring directly at the sun can improve your health. People have a tendency to search out information that confirms their beliefs.[101] They seek confirmation of their mental models. In order to fight the Dunning-Kruger effect, it is also important to seek out arguments that refute your opinions. You must attempt to find *falsification* of your beliefs by seeking out facts that are in opposition to what you think. Assessing the arguments for and against a certain belief will lead to a more objective opinion. Richard Dawkins, a professor of biology at Oxford University says: *"By all means let's be open-minded, but not so open-minded that our brains drop out."*

- **Apply the principle of what is called Occam's razor** – This 700-year-old logic principle states that if there is more than one explanation for a certain phenomenon, it is most likely that the simplest will also be the truest. Were terrorists really responsible for the September 11 attacks? Or was the American government behind an extensive conspiracy in which everything was set up so that it seemed as if terrorists had committed these acts? If we want to make an opinion just according to Occam's razor, the first, less complicated option is more likely to be true. Occam's razor is good for quickly creating initial opinions on matters. In order to obtain greater objectivity, you will always need to search out more reliable information and facts though.

- **Watch out for the mass Dunning-Kruger effect** – In 1978, more than 900 people from the Peoples Temple cult died by committing the largest mass suicide in history.[102] It may be an extreme case, but mass nonobjectivity occurs on a lesser scale very often. Sometimes people with strong personalities subconsciously surround themselves with people who confirm their mental models. They gradually close themselves off in a kind of bubble of nonobjectivity, in which they receive no negative feedback on their ideas. This happens in families as well as in companies. The result is a small group of people who share the same idea about something, unfortunately, one that does not correspond with reality. Mass nonobjectivity is one of the biggest social risks that exist. The nineteenth-century author Julius Zeyer had a relatively uncompromising view of this risk: *"The crowd is always blind."*

- **Don't be dogmatic** - Dogmas, that is, unquestionable truths, are a common source of nonobjectivity. Thus, you should always be willing to admit that your opinions may be wrong. Accept the fact that you might be under the influence of the Dunning-Kruger effect.* If your belief in something is rock solid, try admitting that you may not be right. If, for example Adolf Hitler or Anders Breivik had admitted this to themselves, they might have not gone so far. Nobel laureate André Gide expressed the risks of dogma like this: *"Follow the man who seeks truth; run from the man who has found it."*

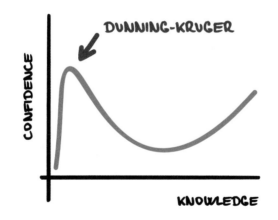

---

*   *Author's note:* I, for example, concede the possibility that this entire book might be nonobjective. If this is so, and someone provides me with better information, I would be glad to re-evaluate my conclusions.

Chapter Recap: Objectivity

Our brains make decisions on the basis of **mental models**.

Mental models represent our notions of how the world around us works.

The fact that someone firmly believes in his or her models doesn't mean they are correct.

We are all subject to the **Dunning-Kruger effect**. We often believe things that aren't true.

The more nonobjective one is, the more flawed decisions one will make.

If you want to work on improving yourself, you need to find areas in which you are not objective.

You can systematically increase your objectivity.

Successfully fighting the Dunning-Kruger effect mainly involves **educating yourself with facts from reliable sources of information**.

Other ways to increase your objectivity include **collecting various types of feedback**, **engaging in critical thinking**, and **questioning your intuition and dogma**.

The nonobjectivity of an individual has the potential to lead to a very dangerous form of **collective nonobjectivity**.

Seeking the truth is a never-ending journey.

I'll be glad to see the day when the Dunning-Kruger effect becomes well-known and frequently discussed. Calling someone an idiot is not helpful. It would be more useful to point out his or her nonobjectivity and to say: "That guy has a DK." When people argue, admitting that they may be suffering from the Dunning-Kruger effect will increase the odds of coming to an agreement and compromising. If more people try to be objective, there will be much less evil in this world caused by nonobjectivity.

On a scale from 1 to 10, how much are you trying to make your mental models more **objective**?

CONCLUSION

THE KEY TO LONGEVITY

Recently, I met with a client with whom I had last consulted more than a year ago. Just by looking at him, he seemed much more balanced than when we used to meet before. Since our last meeting, he had gotten rid of almost all his bad habits as well as learned several new, positive ones.

He told me that he was experiencing one of the happiest times in his life. After many years, he had found something with meaning, something that gets him in a flow state. His chronic procrastination had almost disappeared. Even after a year without counseling, everything was working for him.

What was the secret to his success? How can you transfer the information from this book into everyday practice?

Many training courses and individual counseling sessions end with people returning to their old ways after a few days or weeks. Even after reading self-help books, people tend to quickly forget most of what they have just learned. No long-term changes occur. For many years, I looked for a way to overcome this phenomenon.

I was disturbed by the fact that my brain kept forgetting even the things that were most important for my personal development. My colleagues and I have discovered a method that effectively solves this problem; we call it having a *Meeting with myself.*

TOOL: A Meeting with Myself

The daily grind often doesn't permit you the time to stop and think about your personal growth or about your long-term life plan. People's lives are often just a series of reactions to the outside world that is dragging them along. If you want to move forward, your personal growth must be built on a stable foundation. This is where holding **Meetings with myself** comes into play.

These meetings are based on the idea of *self-coaching*. In classic coaching, a coach poses you a series of questions that are intended to stimulate thought about critical elements of personal growth. In self-coaching, you ask these questions yourself.

You ask yourself how far you have moved forward recently. You consider which direction you would like to head in life. You think about what you can improve even further. On a scale of 1 to 10, you evaluate how well you are using the practical personal development tools you have learned. During your meetings, you can also revisit the theoretical models presented in this book. Finally, you determine specific tasks that you must complete before your next meeting.

How Do "Meetings with Myself" Work?

I suggest you "call" a self-coaching meeting once a week, ideally at a regular time, for example every Sunday at 4:00 p.m. It is also a good idea to select a special place to hold your meeting, such as, for example, your favorite cafe. I wouldn't recommend having this meeting at your desk with your computer—and movies and the Internet—in front of you. If you manage to connect a special place with working on your personal development, the easier it will be for you to make a habit out of these meetings, and they will become a lasting and stable part of your life.

Set aside about an hour for your meeting, sit by yourself, shut off your phone, and take some paper and a pen. During your self-coaching sessions, answer the following questions. Write down your answers and important ideas you have on the paper so that you can review them during later meetings.

Potential Risks?

The greatest risk is putting the meeting off. Use the maximum effort towards making sure you hold these meetings regularly. I recommend scheduling several in advance for the upcoming weeks in your calendar. Always have at least two planned; if one of them doesn't work out then you won't end up breaking your habit.

The next risk is that at first, you won't know exactly how to conduct your meetings or what to write on your paper. One of my clients told me that she put off her meetings because she didn't know what exactly to do during them. This is why we have created a form to help you out. You can find it here: **www.procrastination.com/meeting-with-myself**. You will see that after just a few meetings you will be doing everything almost automatically.

A MEETING WITH YOURSELF:

1) HOW FAR HAVE I MOVED FORWARD SINCE THE LAST MEETING? WHAT HAVE I SUCEEDED AT?

2) HOW FAR WOULD I LIKE TO MOVE FORWARD BY THE TIME OF MY NEXT MEETING? WHAT ASPECT OF MY PERSONAL DEVELOPMENT WOULD I LIKE TO FOCUS ON?

3) HOW WELL HAVE I BEEN USING THE TOOLS?

1..10
- [ ] PERSONAL VISION
- [ ] HABIT-LIST
- [ ] TO-DO TODAY
- [ ] HEROISM

1..10
- [ ] FLOW-LIST
- [ ] INNER-SWITCH
- [ ] HAMSTER-RESTART
- [ ] MEETINGS WITH YOURSELF

4) TO-DO FOR THE NEXT MEETING:

The End of Procrastination and Your New Beginning

The main purpose of this book was to help you understand how procrastination works. At its core, it presents theoretical models and simple practical tools that can help effectively achieve lasting victory over it.

Beating procrastination takes everyday heroism. I hope that this book helps you find greater meaning in life, higher productivity and effectiveness, and lasting happiness as well as a greater level of objectivity. Even if it helps only a fraction of its readers, writing it will have had great meaning for me.

They say repetition is the mother of wisdom for a reason. That's why I recommend you keep turning to this book even after you have read it. You don't need to start reading; just leaf through it. The illustrations will remind you of the main ideas it contains. Even though I present the material contained in this book at workshops several times a week, even after all these years I still find myself discovering new connections. I firmly believe that you too shall succeed in finding new ways to put this information to good use.

I won't be offended at all if this book finds a permanent home next to your toilet. The bathroom is the ideal place for reviewing the key ideas in this book for several minutes every day.*

---

*   *Author's note:* Even if you don't find the pages of this book groundbreaking, you can use them otherwise.

THE MOST IMPORTANT IDEA IN THIS BOOK:

Finally, in conclusion, I'd like to ask a favor of you. Imagine that you had to forget everything you learned about in this book, but that you could remember just one thing. What would that one thing be? Please write it down. I would be glad if you e-mailed it to me: **petr@procrastination.com**. Thank you.

As William James once said: *"The most important thing in life is to live for something more than just your own life."* I hope that the information in this book becomes a useful helper on your journey in life. Now it is up to you. I wish you luck.

THEORY:

FUTURE

PRESENT

1) MOTIVATION
2) DISCIPLINE
3) OUTCOMES
4) OBJECTIVITY

MAIN TOOLS:

1) PERSONAL VISION
2) HABIT-LIST
3) TO-DO TODAY
4) HEROISM
5) FLOW-LIST
6) INNER-SWITCH
7) HAMSTER-RESTART
8) MEETINGS WITH YOURSELF

ADDITIONAL METHODS:

1) PERSONAL SWOT ANALYSIS
2) LIST OF PERSONAL ACHIEVEMENTS
3) ANALYSIS OF MOTIVATIONAL ACTIVITIES
4) BETA VERSION OF YOUR VISION
5) HAMSTER ANALYSIS

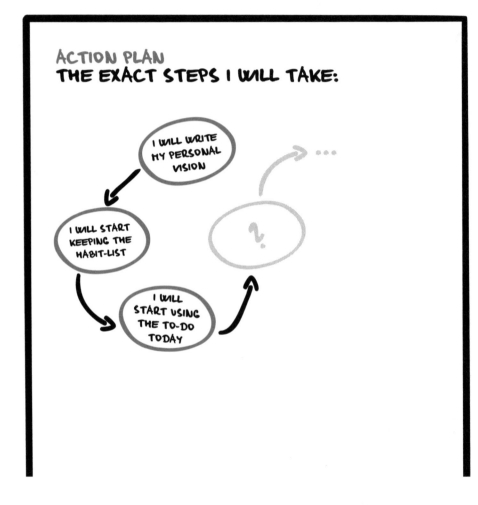

ACTION PLAN
THE EXACT STEPS I WILL TAKE:

I WILL WRITE MY PERSONAL VISION

I WILL START KEEPING THE HABIT-LIST

I WILL START USING THE TO-DO TODAY

?

NOTES

[1]

FERRARI, J. R. Procrastination as self-regulation failure of performance: Effects of cognitive load, self-awareness, and time limits on "working best under pressure". *European Journal of Personality*. 2001, 15th ed., no. 5, pp. 391–406.

BAUMEISTER, R. F. Choking under pressure: Self-consciousness and paradoxical effects of incentives on skillful performance. *Journal of Personality and Social Psychology*. 1984, 46th ed., no. 3, pp. 610–620.

GRAWE, K. *Neuropsychotherapy: How the Neurosciences Inform Effective Psychotherapy.* New Jersey: Routledge, 2007. ISBN 08-058-6122-X.

[2]

HÉSIOD. *Works and days.*

[3]

MORRISON, M. and ROESE, N. Regrets of the typical American: Findings from a nationally representative sample. *Social Psychological and Personality Science*. 2011, 2nd ed., no. 6, pp. 576–583.

[4]

KINSELLA, K. G. Changes in life expectancy 1900–1990. *The American Journal of Clinical Nutrition*. 1992, 55th ed., no. 6, pp. 1196–1202.

GOKLANY, I. M. *The Improving State of the World: Why We're Living Longer, Healthier, More Comfortable Lives on a Cleaner Planet.* Washington, D.C: Cato Institute, 2007. ISBN 19-308-6598-8.

DIAMANDIS, P. H. & KOTLER, S. *Abundance: The Future Is Better Than You Think.* 1st ed., New York: Free Press, 2012. ISBN 14-516-1421-7.

[5]

ABOUHARB, M. R. & KIMBALL, A. L. A new dataset on infant mortality rates, 1816–2002. *Journal of Peace Research*. 2007, 44th ed., no. 6, pp. 743–754.

DIAMANDIS, P. H. & KOTLER, S. *Abundance: The Future Is Better Than You Think.* 1st ed., New York: Free Press, 2012. ISBN 14-516-1421-7.

[6]

KRUG, E. G., MERCY, J. A., DAHLBERG, L. L. & ZWI, A. B. The world report on violence and health. *The Lancet*. 2002, vol. 360, no. 9339, pp. 1083–1088.

PINKER, S. *The Better Angels of Our Nature: Why Violence Has Declined*. New York: Viking, 2011. ISBN 06-700-2315-9.

[7]

MOORE, G. E. (1998). Cramming more components onto integrated circuits. Proceedings of the IEEE, 86(1), pp. 82-85.

HILBERT, M. & LÓPEZ, P. The world's technological capacity to store, communicate, and compute information. *Science*. 2011, no. 6025, pp. 60–65.

[8]

VEENHOVEN, R. Erasmus University Rotterdam. *World Database of Happiness* [online]. 2012 [qt. 2013-03-24]. web: http://worlddatabaseofhappiness.eur.nl

SHIN, D. C. Does rapid economic growth improve the human lot? Some empirical evidence. *Social Indicators Research*. London: Published for the British Council and the National Book League by Longmans, Green, 1980, 8th ed., no. 2, pp. 199–221.

GALLUP. *Gallup.Com: Daily News, Polls, Public Opinion on Politics, Economy, Wellbeing, and World* [online]. 2013, 2013-03-24 [qt. 2013-03-24]. web: http://www.gallup.com

[9]

REDELMEIER, D. A. Medical decision making in situations that offer multiple alternatives. *The Journal of the American Medical Association*. 1995, 273rd ed., no. 4, pp. 302–305.

ARIELY, D. & LEVAV, J. Sequential choice in group settings: Taking the road less traveled and less enjoyed. *Journal of Consumer Research*. 2000, 27th ed., no. 3, pp. 279–290.

IYENGAR, S. S., HUBERMAN, G. & JIANG, G. How much choice is too much?: Contributions to 401(k) retirement plans. *Pension Design and Structure: New Lessons from Behavioral Finance*. 2005.

IYENGAR, S. S. & LEPPER, M. R. Rethinking the value of choice: A cultural perspective on intrinsic motivation. *Journal of Personality and Social Psychology*. 1999, 76th ed., no. 3, pp. 349–366.

IYENGAR, S. S., WELLS, R. E. & SCHWARTZ, B. Doing better but feeling worse: Looking for the "best" job undermines satisfaction. *Psychological Science*. 2006, 17th ed., no. 2, pp. 143–150.

SCHWARTZ, B. *The Paradox of Choice: Why More Is Less*. Reissued. New York: Harper Perennial, 2005. ISBN 978-006-0005-696.

IYENGAR, S. S. *The Art of Choosing*. 1st ed., New York: Twelve, 2010. ISBN 978-044-6504-119.

[10]

IYENGAR, S. S. & LEPPER, M. R. When choice is demotivating: Can one desire too much of a good thing? *Journal of Personality and Social Psychology*. 2000, 79th ed., no. 6, pp. 995–1006.

IYENGAR, S. S., HUBERMAN, G. & JIANG, G. How much choice is too much?: Contributions to 401(k) retirement plans. *Pension Design and Structure: New Lessons from Behavioral Finance*. 2005.

SCHWARTZ, B. *The Paradox of Choice: Why More Is Less*. Reissued. New York: Harper Perennial, 2005. ISBN 978-006-0005-696.

IYENGAR, S. S. *The Art of Choosing*. 1st ed., New York: Twelve, 2010. ISBN 978-044-6504-119.

[11]

IYENGAR, S. S. & LEPPER, M. R. When choice is demotivating: Can one desire too much of a good thing? *Journal of Personality and Social Psychology*. 2000, 79th ed., no. 6, pp. 995–1006.

IYENGAR, S. S., HUBERMAN, G. & JIANG, G. How much choice is too much?: Contributions to 401(k) retirement plans. *Pension Design and Structure: New Lessons from Behavioral Finance*. 2005.

REDELMEIER, D. A. Medical decision making in situations that offer multiple alternatives. *The Journal of the American Medical Association*. 1995, 273rd ed., no. 4, pp. 302–305.

SCHWARTZ, B. *The Paradox of Choice: Why More Is Less*. Reissued. New York: Harper Perennial, 2005. ISBN 978-006-0005-696.

IYENGAR, S. S. *The Art of Choosing*. 1st Ed. New York: Twelve, 2010. ISBN 978-044-6504-119.

[12]

GILBERT, D. T. & EBERT, J. E. Decisions and revisions: the affective forecasting of changeable outcomes. *Journal of Personality and Social Psychology*. 2002, 82nd ed., no. 4, pp. 503–514.

IYENGAR, S. S., WELLS, R. E. & SCHWARTZ, B. Doing better but feeling worse: Looking for the "best" job undermines satisfaction. *Psychological Science*. 2006, 17th ed., no. 2, pp. 143–150.

SCHWARTZ, B. *The Paradox of Choice: Why More Is Less*. Reissued. New York: Harper Perennial, 2005. ISBN 978-006-0005-696.

IYENGAR, S. S. *The Art of Choosing*. 1st ed. New York: Twelve, 2010. ISBN 978-044-6504-119.

[13]

SCHWARTZ, B. *The Paradox of Choice: Why More Is Less*. Reissued. New York: Harper Perennial, 2005. ISBN 978-006-0005-696.

IYENGAR, S. S. *The Art of Choosing*. 1st ed., New York: Twelve, 2010. ISBN 978-044-6504-119.

ARIELY, D. *Predictably Irrational: The Hidden Forces That Shape Our Decisions*. 1st ed., New York: Harper Perennial, 2010. ISBN 978-006-1353-246.

[14]

BERRIDGE, K. C. & KRINGELBACH, M. L. Affective neuroscience of pleasure: reward in humans and animals. *Psychopharmacology*. 2008, no. 3, pp. 457–480.

CSÍKSZENTMIHÁLYI, M. *Finding Flow: The Psychology of Engagement with Everyday Life*. 1st ed., New York: Basic Books, 1997. ISBN 04-650-2411-4.

CSÍKSZENTMIHÁLYI, M. *Flow: The Psychology of Optimal Experience*. New York: HarperPerennial, 1991. ISBN 00-609-2043-2.

[15]

THOMSON REUTERS. *Web of Knowledge: Discovery Starts Here* [online]. 2013, 2013-03-24 [qt. 2013-03-24]. web: http://www.webofknowledge.com

[16]

Where can I find the Yale study from 1953 about goal-setting? In: *University of Pennsylvania Library* [online]. 2002 [qt. 2013-03-24]. web: http://faq.library.yale.edu/recordDetail?id=7508

TABAK, L. If your goal is success, don't consult these gurus. In: *Fast Company* [online]. 1996-12-31 [qt. 2013-03-24]. web: http://www.fastcompany.com/27953/if-your-goal-success-dont-consult-these-gurus

[17]

WARE, C. *Information Visualization: Perception for Design*. 3rd ed., Morgan Kaufmann, 2012. ISBN 978-012-3814-647.

[18]

ARIAS-CARRIÓN, O. & PÖPPEL, E. Dopamine, learning, and reward-seeking behavior. *Acta Neurobiol Exp.* 2007, 67th ed., no. 4.

BERRIDGE, K. C. & KRINGELBACH, M. L. Affective neuroscience of pleasure: reward in humans and animals. *Psychopharmacology.* 2008, 3rd ed., pp. 457–480.

KRINGELBACH, M. L. The functional neuroanatomy of pleasure and happiness. *Discovery Medicine.* 2010, Year. 9, 49th ed., pp. 579–587.

LINDEN, D. J. *The Compass of Pleasure: How Our Brains Make Fatty Foods, Orgasm, Exercise, Marijuana, Generosity, Vodka, Learning, and Gambling Feel So Good.* New York: Viking, 2011. ISBN 06-700-2258-6.

[19]

NOVO NORDISK. *Novo Nordisk annual report 2015* [online]. web: https://www.novonordisk.com/content/dam/Denmark/HQ/Commons/documents/Novo-Nordisk-Annual-Report-2015.PDF

[20]

ARIELY, D., KAMENICA, E. & PRELEC, D. Man's search for meaning: The case of Legos. *Journal of Economic Behavior and Organization.* 2008, 67th ed., no. 3–4, pp. 671–677.

[21]

ARIAS-CARRIÓN, O. & PÖPPEL, E. Dopamine, learning, and reward-seeking behavior. *Acta Neurobiol Exp.* 2007, 67th ed., no. 4.

ACHOR, S. Positive intelligence. *Harward Business Review.* 2012, 90th ed., no. 1–2, pp. 100–102.

ASHBY, F. G., ISEN, A. M. & TURKEN, A. U. A neuropsychological theory of positive affect and its influence on cognition. *Psychological Review.* 1999, 106th ed., no. 3.

ISEN, A. M. *Psychological and Biological Approaches to Emotion.* Hillsdale, N. J.: L. Erlbaum Associates, 1990, pp. 75–94. ISBN 978-080-5801-507.

ACHOR, S. *The Happiness Advantage: The Seven Principles of Positive Psychology That Fuel Success and Performance at Work.* 1st ed., New York: Broadway Books, 2010. ISBN 978-030-7591-548.

[22]

HOWES, M. J., HOKANSON, J. E. & LOEWENSTEIN, D. A. Induction of depressive affect after prolonged exposure to a mildly depressed individual. *Journal of Personality and Social Psychology.* 1985, 49th ed., no. 4.

CHRISTAKIS, N. A. & FOWLER, J. H. Dynamic spread of happiness in a large social network: longitudinal analysis over 20 years in the Framingham Heart Study. *British Medical Journal.* 2008, no. 337.

HILL, A. L., RAND, D. G., NOWAK, M. A. & CHRISTAKIS, N. A. Emotions as infectious diseases in a large social network: the SISa model. *Proceedings of the Royal Society B: Biological Sciences.* 2010, 277th ed., no. 1701, pp. 3827–3835.

CHRISTAKIS, N. A. & FOWLER, J. H. *Connected: The Surprising Power of Our Social Networks and How They Shape Our Lives: How Your Friends' Friends' Friends Affect Everything You Feel, Think, and Do.* 1st ed., New York: Back Bay Books, 2009. ISBN 978-031-6036-139.

[23]

LEPPER, M. R., GREENE, D. & NISBETT, R. E. Undermining children's intrinsic interest with extrinsic reward: A test of the "overjustification" hypothesis. *Journal of Personality and Social Psychology.* 1973, 28th ed., no. 1, pp. 129–137.

HEYMAN, J. & ARIELY, D. Effort for payment: A tale of two markets. *Psychological Science.* 2004, 15th ed., no. 11, pp. 787–793.

ARIELY, D., GNEEZY, U., LOEWENSTEIN, G. & MAZAR, N. Large stakes and big mistakes. *Review of Economic Studies.* 2009, 76th ed., no. 2, pp. 451–469.

GLUCKSBERG, S. The influence of strength of drive on functional fixedness and perceptual recognition. *Journal of Experimental Psychology.* 1962, 63rd ed., no. 1, pp. 36–41.

PINK, D. H. *Drive: The Surprising Truth About What Motivates Us.* 1st ed., New York: Riverhead Books, 2011. ISBN 978-159-4484-803.

[24]

LEPPER, M. R., GREENE, D. & NISBETT, R. E. Undermining children's intrinsic interest with extrinsic reward: A test of the " overjustification" hypothesis. *Journal of Personality and Social Psychology.* 1973, 28the, no. 1, pp. 129–137.

GNEEZY, U. & RUSTICHINI, A. A. Fine is a price. *The Journal of Legal Studies.* 2000, 29th ed., no. 1, pp. 1–17.

PINK, D. H. *Drive: The Surprising Truth About What Motivates Us.* 1st ed., New York: Riverhead Books, 2011. ISBN 978-159-4484-803.

ARIELY, D. *The Upside of Irrationality: The Unexpected Benefits of Defying Logic.* 1st ed., New York: HarperPerennial, 2011. ISBN 978-006-1995-040.

[25]

LEPPER, M. R., GREENE, D. & NISBETT, R. E. Undermining children's intrinsic interest with extrinsic reward: A test of the "overjustification" hypothesis. *Journal of Personality and Social Psychology.* 1973, 28th ed., pp. 129–137.

PINK, D. H. *Drive: The Surprising Truth About What Motivates Us.* 1st ed., New York: Riverhead Books, 2011. ISBN 978-159-4484-803.

[26]

KEELY, L. C. Why isn't growth making us happier? Utility on the hedonic treadmill. *Journal of Economic Behavior.* 2005, 57th ed., no. 3, pp. 333–355.

LYUBOMIRSKY, S., SHELDON, K. M. & SCHKADE, D. Pursuing happiness: The architecture of sustainable change. 2005, UC Riverside.

SHELDON, K. M. & LYUBOMIRSKY, S. Achieving sustainable gains in happiness: Change your actions, not your circumstances. *Journal of Happiness Studies.* 2006, 7th ed., no. 1, pp. 55–86.

ARIELY, D. *The Upside of Irrationality: The Unexpected Benefits of Defying Logic.* 1st ed., New York: HarperPerennial, 2011. ISBN 978-006-1995-040.

PINK, D. H. *Drive: The Surprising Truth About What Motivates Us.* 1st ed., New York: Riverhead Books, 2011. ISBN 978-159-4484-803.

[27]

NESTLER, E. J. The neurobiology of cocaine addiction. *Science & Practice Perspectives.* 2005, 3rd ed., no. 1, pp. 4–10.

BERRIDGE, K. C. & KRINGELBACH, M. L. Affective neuroscience of pleasure: reward in humans and animals. *Psychopharmacology.* 2008, no. 3, pp. 457–480.

SUVOROV, A. Addiction to rewards. Toulouse School of Economics, 2003.

KRINGELBACH, M. L. The functional neuroanatomy of pleasure and happiness. *Discovery Medicine.* 2010, 9th ed., no. 49, pp. 579–587.

LINDEN, D. J. *The Compass of Pleasure: How Our Brains Make Fatty Foods, Orgasm, Exercise, Marijuana, Generosity, Vodka, Learning, and Gambling Feel So Good.* New York: Viking, 2011. ISBN 06-700-2258-6.

[28]

MILLER, E. K., FREEDMAN, D. J. & WALLIS, J. D. The prefrontal cortex: categories, concepts and cognition. *Philosophical Transactions of the Royal Society B: Biological Sciences*. 2002-08-29, 357th ed., no. 1424, pp. 1123–1136.

GILBERT, D. T. *Stumbling on Happiness*. 1st ed., New York: A. A. Knopf, 2006. ISBN 14-000-4266-6.

[29]

GILBERT, D. T. *Stumbling on Happiness*. 1st ed., New York: A. A. Knopf, 2006. ISBN 14-000-4266-6.

[30]

LÖVHEIM, H. A new three-dimensional model for emotions and monoamine neurotransmitters. *Medical Hypotheses*. 2012, 78th ed., no. 2, pp. 341–348.

SCHNEIDER, T. A., BUTRYN, T. M., FURST, D. M. & MASUCCI, M. A. A qualitative examination of risk among elite adventure racers. *Journal of Sport Behavior*. 2007, 30th ed., no. 3.

SELIGMAN, M. E. P. *Authentic Happiness: Using the New Positive Psychology to Realize Your Potential for Lasting Fulfillment*. 1st ed., New York: Free, 2002. ISBN 978-074-3222-983.

[31]

KEELY, L. C. Why isn't growth making us happier? Utility on the hedonic treadmill. *Journal of Economic Behavior*. 2005, 57th ed., no. 3, pp. 333–355.

KAHNEMAN, D. & KRUEGER, A. B. Developments in the measurement of subjective well-being. *The Journal of Economic Perspectives*, 2006, 20th ed., no. 1, pp. 3–24.

LYUBOMIRSKY, S., SHELDON, K. M. & SCHKADE, D. Pursuing happiness: The architecture of sustainable change. 2005, UC Riverside.

SCHNEIDER, T. A., BUTRYN, T. M., FURST, D. M. & MASUCCI, M. A. A qualitative examination of risk among elite adventure racers. *Journal of Sport Behavior*. 2007, 30th ed., no. 3.

GILBERT, D. T. *Stumbling on Happiness*. 1st ed., New York: A. A. Knopf, 2006. ISBN 14-000-4266-6.

DIENER, E., LUCAS, R. E. & SCOLLON, C. N. Beyond the hedonic treadmill: Revising the adaptation theory of well-being. In: DIENER, E. *The Science of Well-Being*. New York: Springer Netherlands, 2009, pp. 103–118. ISBN 978-90-481-2349-0.

ARIELY, D. *The Upside of Irrationality: The Unexpected Benefits of Defying Logic.* 1st ed., New York: HarperPerennial, 2011. ISBN 978-006-1995-040.

[32]

BRICKMAN, P., COATES, D. & JANOFF-BULMAN, R. Lottery winners and accident victims: Is happiness relative? *Journal of Personality and Social Psychology.* 1978, 36th ed., no. 8, pp. 917–927.

KAHNEMAN, D. & KRUEGER, A. B. Developments in the measurement of subjective well-being. *The Journal of Economic Perspectives*, 2006, 20th ed., no. 1, pp. 3–24.

DI TELLA, R., HAISKEN-DE NEW, J. & MACCULLOCH, R. Happiness adaptation to income and to status in an individual panel. *Journal of Economic Behavior.* 2010, 76th ed., no. 3, pp. 834–852.

HULME, O. Comparative neurobiology: Hedonics & Happiness. University of British Columbia. 2010.

ARIELY, D. *The Upside of Irrationality: The Unexpected Benefits of Defying Logic.* 1st ed., New York: HarperPerennial, 2011. ISBN 978-006-1995-040.

[33]

BRICKMAN, P., COATES, D. & JANOFF-BULMAN, R. Lottery winners and accident victims: is happiness relative? *Journal of Personality and Social Psychology.* 1978, 36th ed., no. 8, pp. 917–927.

[34]

EASTERLIN, R. A. Income and happiness: Towards a unified theory. *The Economic Journal.* 2001, 111th ed., no. 473, pp. 465–484.

DI TELLA, R., HAISKEN-DE NEW, J. & MACCULLOCH, R. Happiness adaptation to income and to status in an individual panel. *Journal of Economic Behavior.* 2010, 76th ed., no. 3, pp. 834–852.

[35]

NESTLER, E. J. The neurobiology of cocaine addiction. *Science & Practice Perspectives.* 2005, 3rd ed., no. 1, pp. 4–10.

BERRIDGE, K. C. & KRINGELBACH, M. L. Affective neuroscience of pleasure: reward in humans and animals. *Psychopharmacology.* 2008, no. 3, pp. 457–480.

SUVOROV, A. Addiction to rewards. Toulouse School of Economics, 2003.

KRINGELBACH, M. L. The functional neuroanatomy of pleasure and happiness. *Discovery Medicine*. 2010, 9th ed., no. 49, pp. 579–587.

LINDEN, D. J. *The Compass of Pleasure: How Our Brains Make Fatty Foods, Orgasm, Exercise, Marijuana, Generosity, Vodka, Learning, and Gambling Feel So Good*. New York: Viking, 2011. ISBN 06-700-2258-6.

[36]

BERRIDGE, K. C. & KRINGELBACH, M. L. Affective neuroscience of pleasure: reward in humans and animals. *Psychopharmacology*. 2008, no. 3, pp. 457–480.

SUVOROV, A. Addiction to rewards. Toulouse School of Economics, 2003.

[37]

NOVO NORDISK. *Changing Diabetes* [online]. [qt. 2013-03-25]. Web: http://www.novonordisk.com/about-novo-nordisk/changing-diabetes.html

[38]

YOUNG, J. A. & MICHELLE, M. The zone: Evidence of a universal phenomenon for athletes across sports. *Athletic Insight: The Online Journal of Sport Psychology*. 1999, 1st ed., no. 3, pp. 21–30.

CSÍKSZENTMIHÁLYI, M. *Optimal Experience: Psychological Studies of Flow in Consciousness*. 1st ed. Cambridge: Cambridge University Press, 1992. ISBN 978-052-1438-094.

JACKSON, S. A & CSÍKSZENTMIHÁLYI, M. *Flow in Sports*. Champaign, IL: Human Kinetics, 1999. ISBN 08-801-1876-8.

CSÍKSZENTMIHÁLYI, M. *Flow: The Psychology of Optimal Experience*. 1st ed., New York: Harper Perennial, 2008. ISBN 978-006-0162-535.

CSÍKSZENTMIHÁLYI, M. *Beyond Boredom and Anxiety*. 1st ed., San Francisco: Jossey-Bass Publishers, 1975. ISBN 08-758-9261-2.

CSÍKSZENTMIHÁLYI, M. *Finding Flow: The Psychology of Engagement with Everyday Life*. 1st ed., New York: Basic Books, 2008. ISBN 978-046-5024-117.

CSÍKSZENTMIHÁLYI, M. *Creativity: Flow and the Psychology of Discovery and Invention*. 1st ed., New York: HarperCollins Publishers, 1997. ISBN 978-006-0928-209.

[39]

CSÍKSZENTMIHÁLYI, M. *Flow: The Psychology of Optimal Experience*. 1st ed., New York: Harper Perennial, 2008. ISBN 978-006-0162-535.

CSÍKSZENTMIHÁLYI, M. *Beyond Boredom and Anxiety.* 1st ed., San Francisco: Jossey-Bass Publishers, 1975. ISBN 08-758-9261-2.

CSÍKSZENTMIHÁLYI, M. *Finding Flow: The Psychology of Engagement with Everyday Life.* 1st ed., New York: BasicBooks, 2008. ISBN 978-046-5024-117.

CSÍKSZENTMIHÁLYI, M. *Creativity: Flow and the Psychology of Discovery and Invention.* 1st ed., New York: HarperCollins Publishers, 1997. ISBN 978-006-0928-209.

[40]

WILSON, E. O. *The Social Conquest of Earth.* 1st ed., New York: Liveright Pub. Corporation, 2012. ISBN 978-087-1404-138.

[41]

WILSON, E. O. *The Social Conquest of Earth.* 1st ed., New York: Liveright Pub. Corporation, 2012. ISBN 978-087-1404-138.

[42]

WILSON, E. O. *The Social Conquest of Earth.* 1st ed., New York: Liveright Pub. Corporation, 2012. ISBN 978-087-1404-138.

[43]

RIDLEY, M. *The Origins of Virtue: Human Instincts and the Evolution of Cooperation.* London: Penguin Books, 1998. ISBN 978-014-0264-456.

RIDLEY, M. *The Red Queen: Sex and the Evolution of Human Nature.* 1st ed., New York: Perennial, 2003. ISBN 00-605-5657-9.

[44]

DARWIN, C. *The Descent of Man and Selection in Relation to Sex.* London: Penguin, 2004. ISBN 978-014-0436-310.

RUSE, M. Charles Darwin and group selection. *Annals of Science.* 1980, 37th ed., no. 6, pp. 615–630.

[45]

WRIGHT, R. *NonZero: The Logic of Human Destiny.* 1st ed., New York: Pantheon Books, 2000. ISBN 06-794-4252-9.

WRIGHT, R. *The Evolution of God.* 1st ed., New York: Little, Brown, 2009. ISBN 03-167-3491-8.

VON NEUMANN, J. *Theory of Games and Economic Behavior*. 16th ed., Princeton: Princeton University Press, 2004. ISBN 06-911-1993-7.

John F. NASH, Jr. – Autobiography. *The Official Web Site of the Nobel Prize* [online]. 1995 [qt. 2013-03-25]. web: http://www.nobelprize.org/nobel_prizes/economics/laureates/1994/nash.html

[46]

HAIDT, J. *The Righteous Mind: Why Good People Are Divided by Politics and Religion* Vintage, 2nd ed., 2103. ISBN 978-0307455772.

[47]

SHIN, J. & ARIELY, D. Keeping doors open: The effect of unavailability on incentives to keep options viable. *Management Science*. 2004, 50th ed., no. 5, pp. 575–586.

SCHWARTZ, B. *The Paradox of Choice: Why More Is Less*. Reissued. New York: Harper Perennial, 2005. ISBN 978-006-0005-696.

IYENGAR, S. S. *The Art of Choosing*. 1st ed., New York: Twelve, 2010. ISBN 978-044-6504-119.

[48]

STEEL, P. The nature of procrastination: A meta-analytic and theoretical review of quintessential self-regulatory failure. *Psychological Bulletin*. 2007, 133rd ed., no. 1, pp. 65–94.

[49]

SCHOENEMANN, P. T. Evolution of the size and functional areas of the human brain. *Annual Review of Anthropology*. 2006, 35th ed., no. 1, pp. 379–406.

SEMENDEFERI, K., DAMASIO, H., FRANK, R. & VAN HOESEN, G. W. The evolution of the frontal lobes: a volumetric analysis based on three-dimensional reconstructions of magnetic resonance scans of human and ape brains. *Journal of Human Evolution*. 1997, no. 32, pp. 375–388.

BANYAS, C. A. Evolution and phylogenetic history of the frontal lobes. In: MILLER, B. L. & CUMMINGS, J. L. *The Human Frontal Lobes: Functions and Disorders*. New York: Guilford Press, 1999, pp. 83–106. Science and practice of neuropsychology series. ISBN 978-157-2303-904.

[50]

MACLEAN, P. D. *The Triune Brain in Evolution: Role in Paleocerebral Functions.* New York: Plenum Press, 1990. ISBN 03-064-3168-8.

[51]

LEDOUX, J. *The Emotional Brain: The Mysterious Underpinnings of Emotional Life.* 1st ed., New York: Simon, 1998. ISBN 978-068-4836-591.

LIDZ, C. S. *Early Childhood Assessment.* New York: John Wiley, 2003. ISBN 04-714-1984-2.

DU PLESSIS, E. *The Branded Mind: What Neuroscience Really Tells Us About the Puzzle of the Brain and the Brand.* Philadelphia: Kogan Page, 2011. ISBN 07-494-6298-1.

[52]

MASCARÓ, J. *The Dhammapada: The Path of Perfection.* Harmondsworth: Penguin, 1973. ISBN 01-404-4284-7.

HAIDT, J. *The Happiness Hypothesis: Finding Modern Truth in Ancient Wisdom.* New York: Basic Books, 2006. ISBN 04-650-2801-2.

STEEL, P. *The Procrastination Equation: How to Stop Putting Things Off and Start Getting Stuff Done.* 1st ed., New York: Harper, 2011. ISBN 00-617-0361-3.

[53]

BAUMEISTER, R. F., MURAVEN, M. & TICE, D. M. Ego depletion: A resource model of volition, self-regulation, and controlled processing. *Social Cognition*, 2000, 18th ed., no. 2, pp. 130–150.

HAGGER, M. S., WOOD, C., STIFF, C. & CHATZISARANTIS, N. L. D. Ego depletion and the strength model of self-control: A meta-analysis. *Psychological Bulletin*. 2010, 136th ed., no. 4, pp. 495–525.

BAUMEISTER, R. F., BRATSLAVSKY, E., MURAVEN, M. & TICE, D. M. Ego depletion: Is the active self a limited resource? *Journal of Personality and Social Psychology*. 1998, 74th ed., no. 5, pp. 1252–1265.

BAUMEISTER, R. F. Ego depletion and self-regulation failure: A resource model of self-control. *Alcoholism: Clinical*. 2003, 27th ed., no. 2, pp. 281–284.

BAUMEISTER, R. F. *Handbook of Self-Regulation: Research, Theory, and Applications.* New York: Guilford Press, 2007. ISBN 978-159-3854-751.

STEEL, P. *The Procrastination Equation: How to Stop Putting Things Off and Start Getting Stuff Done*. 1st ed., New York: Harper, 2011. ISBN 00-617-0361-3.

[54]

Newer studies that tried to validate the findings regarding the cognitive resource limitations didn't replicate. Still, there is a meta-analysis that supports it, and research shows that our ability to self-regulate is based on simple sugars, which level is depletable. Therefore, the issue with cognitive resource and its limitations will require further research.

[55]

GAILLIOT, M. T., BAUMEISTER, R. F., DEWALL, C. N., MANER, J. K., PLANT, E. A., TICE, D. M., BREWER, L. E. & SCHMEICHEL, B. J. Self-control relies on glucose as a limited energy source: Willpower is more than a metaphor. *Journal of Personality and Social Psychology*. 2007, 92nd ed., no. 2, pp. 325–336.

FAIRCLOUGH, S. H. & HOUSTON, K. A metabolic measure of mental effort. *Biological Psychology*, 2004, 66th ed., no. 2, pp. 177–190.

[56]

BAUMEISTER, R. F., BRATSLAVSKY, E., MURAVEN, M. & TICE, D. M. Ego depletion: Is the active self a limited resource? *Journal of Personality and Social Psychology*. 1998, 74th ed., no. 5, pp. 1252–1265.

BAUMEISTER, R. F. Ego depletion and self-regulation failure: A resource model of self-control. *Alcoholism: Clinical*. 2003, 27th ed., no. 2, pp. 281–284.

TICE, D. M., BAUMEISTER, R. F., SHMUELI, D. & MURAVEN, M. Restoring the self: Positive affect helps improve self-regulation following ego depletion. *Journal of Experimental Social Psychology*. 2007, 43rd ed., no. 3, pp. 379–384.

BAUMEISTER, R. F. *Handbook of Self-Regulation: Research, Theory, and Applications*. New York: Guilford Press, 2007. ISBN 978-159-3854-751.

[57]

BARTON, J., & PRETTY, J., *What is the best dose of nature and green exercise for improving mental health? A multi-study analysis.* Environmental science & technology, 44th Ed., pp. 3947-3955.

[58]

HAGGER, M. S., WOOD, C., STIFF C. & CHATZISARANTIS, N. L. D. Ego depletion and the strength model of self-control: A meta-analysis. *Psychological Bulletin.* 2010, 136th ed., no. 4, pp. 495–525.

BAUMEISTER, R. F., BRATSLAVSKY, E., MURAVEN, M. & TICE, D. M. Ego depletion: Is the active self a limited resource? *Journal of Personality and Social Psychology.* 1998, 74th ed., no. 5, pp. 1252–1265.

MEAD, N. L., BAUMEISTER, R. F., GINO, F., SCHWEITZER, M. E. & ARIELY, D. Too tired to tell the truth: Self-control resource depletion and dishonesty. *Journal of Experimental Social Psychology.* 2009, 45th ed., no. 3, pp. 594–597.

BAUMEISTER, R. F. & TIERNEY, J. *Willpower Rediscovering the Greatest Human Strength.* London: Penguin Books, 2012. ISBN 978-014-3122-234.

BAUMEISTER, R. F. *Handbook of Self-Regulation: Research, Theory, and Applications.* New York: Guilford Press, 2007. ISBN 978-159-3854-751.

[59]

LALLY, P., VAN JAARSVELD, C. H. M., POTTS, H. W. W. & WARDLE, J. How are habits formed: Modelling habit formation in the real world. *European Journal of Social Psychology.* 2010, 40th ed., no. 6, pp. 998–1009.

[60]

MAURER, R. & HIRSCHMAN, L. A. *The Spirit of Kaizen: Creating Lasting Excellence One Small Step at a Time.* New York: McGraw-Hill, 2013. ISBN 00-717-9617-7.

IMAI, M. *Kaizen: The Key to Japan's Competitive Success.* 1st ed. New York: McGraw-Hill, 1986. ISBN 00-755-4332-X.

[61]

IYENGAR, S. S. & LEPPER, M. R. When choice is demotivating: Can one desire too much of a good thing? *Journal of Personality and Social Psychology.* 2000, 79th ed., no. 6, pp. 995–1006.

SCHWARTZ, B., WARD, A., MONTEROSSO, J., LYUBOMIRSKY, S., WHITE, K. & LEHMAN, D. R. Maximizing versus satisficing: Happiness is a matter of choice. *Journal of Personality and Social Psychology.* 2002, 83rd, no. 5, pp. 1178–1197.

BROCAS, I. & CARRILLO, J. D. *The Psychology of Economic Decisions.* 2nd ed., New York: Oxford University Press, 2003-2004. ISBN 0-19-925108-8.

SCHWARTZ, B. *The Paradox of Choice: Why More Is Less*. Reissued. New York: Harper Perennial, 2005. ISBN 978-006-0005-696.

IYENGAR, S. S. *The Art of Choosing*. 1st ed., New York: Twelve, 2010. ISBN 978-044-6504-119.

[62]

IYENGAR, S. S., HUBERMAN, G. & JIANG, G. How much choice is too much?: Contributions to 401(k) retirement plans. *Pension Design and Structure: New Lessons from Behavioral Finance.* 2005.

[63]

REDELMEIER, D. A. Medical decision making in situations that offer multiple alternatives. *The Journal of the American Medical Association*. 1995, 273rd ed., no. 4, pp. 302–305.

[64]

GILBERT, D. T. & EBERT, J. E. Decisions and revisions: the affective forecasting of changeable outcomes. *Journal of Personality and Social Psychology*. 2002, 82nd ed., no. 4, pp. 503–514.

IYENGAR, S. S., WELLS, R. E. & SCHWARTZ, B. Doing better but feeling worse: Looking for the "best" job undermines satisfaction. *Psychological Science*. 2006, 17th ed., no. 2, pp. 143–150.

SCHWARTZ, B. *The Paradox of Choice: Why More Is Less*. Reissued. New York: Harper Perennial, 2005. ISBN 978-006-0005-696.

IYENGAR, S. S. *The Art of Choosing*. 1st ed., New York: Twelve, 2010. ISBN 978-044-6504-119.

[65]

GILBERT, D. T. & EBERT, J. E. Decisions and revisions: the affective forecasting of changeable outcomes. *Journal of Personality and Social Psychology*. 2002, 82nd ed., no. 4, pp. 503–514.

[66]

MILLER, G. A. The magical number seven, plus or minus two: some limits on our capacity for processing information. *Psychological Review*. 1956, 63rd ed., no. 2, pp. 81–97.

HALFORD, G. S. (and others). How many variables can humans process? *Psychological Science*, 2005, 16th ed., no. 1, pp. 70–76.

[67]

HANEY, C., BANKS, W. C. & ZIMBARDO, P. G. Study of prisoners and guards in a simulated prison. *Naval Research Reviews*, 1973, no. 9, pp. 1–17.

ZIMBARDO, P. G., MASLACH, C. & HANEY, C. Reflections on the Stanford Prison Experiment: Genesis, transformations, consequences. In: BLASS, T. (Ed.), *Obedience to Authority: Current Perspectives on the Milgram Paradigm,* 2000, pp. 193–237.

HANEY, C. a col. Interpersonal dynamics in a simulated prison. *International Journal of Criminology and Penology,* 1973, no. 1, pp. 69–97.

ZIMBARDO, P. G. *The Stanford Prison Experiment* [online]. 1999, 2013 [qt. 2013-03-25]. Web: http://www.prisonexp.org

ZIMBARDO, P. G. *The Lucifer Effect: Understanding How Good People Turn Evil.* New York: Random House Trade Paperbacks, 2008. ISBN 978-081-2974-447.

[68]

ZIMBARDO, P. G. *The Lucifer Effect: Understanding How Good People Turn Evil.* New York: Random House Trade Paperbacks, 2008. ISBN 978-081-2974-447.

ZIMBARDO, P. G. Power turns good soldiers into "bad apples". *The Boston Globe* [online]. 2004-05-09 [qt. 2013-03-25]. Web: http://archive.boston.com/news/globe/editorial_opinion/oped/articles/2004/05/09/power_turns_good_soldiers_into_bad_apples/

ZIMBARDO, P. G. & O'BRIEN, S. Researcher: It's not bad apples, it's the barrel. *CNN.com* [online]. 2004-05-21 [qt. 2013-03-25]. Web: http://edition.cnn.com/2004/US/05/21/zimbarbo.access/

ZAGORIN, A. Shell-shocked at Abu Ghraib? *TIME Magazine* [online]. 2007-05-18 [qt. 2013-03-25]. Web: http://www.time.com/time/nation/article/0,8599,1622881,00.html

[69]

ZIMBARDO, P. G. A situationist perspective on the psychology of evil: Understanding how good people are transformed into perpetrators. In: MILLER, A. G. (Ed.). *The Social Psychology of Good and Evil.* New York: Guilford Press, 2005, pp. 21–50. ISBN 978-159-3851-941.

ZIMBARDO, P. G. *The Lucifer Effect: Understanding How Good People Turn Evil.* New York: Random House Trade Paperbacks, 2008. ISBN 978-081-2974-447.

[70]

ZIMBARDO, P. G. *The Lucifer Effect: Understanding How Good People Turn Evil.* New York: Random House Trade Paperbacks, 2008. ISBN 978-081-2974-447.

ZIMBARDO, P. G. & FRANCO, Z. Celebrating heroism. *The Lucifer Effect* [online]. 2006, 2013 [qt. 2013-03-25]. Web: http://www.lucifereffect.com/heroism.htm

[71]

Zimbardo is not the only one that reached this conclusion, the conformity of the comfort zone is well established and supported by other research. For example by Salomon Asch and others.

ASCH, S. E. (1956). Studies of independence and conformity: I. A minority of one against a unanimous majority. Psychological monographs: General and applied, 70(9), 1.

BOND, R., & SMITH, P. B. (1996). Culture and conformity: A meta-analysis of studies using Asch's (1952b, 1956) line judgment task. Psychological bulletin, 119(1), 111.

LATANÉ, B., & DARLEY, J. M. (1970). The Unresponsive Bystander: Why Doesn't He Help?, Century Psychology Series. New York,: Appleton-Century Crofts.

CHEKROUN, P., & BRAUER, M. (2002). The bystander effect and social control behavior: The effect of the presence of others on people's reactions to norm violations. European Journal of Social Psychology, 32(6), 853-867.

[72]

BROWN, M. Comfort zone: Model or metaphor? *Australian Journal of Outdoor Education*. 2008, 12th ed., no. 1, pp. 3–12.

BERRIDGE, K. C. & KRINGELBACH, M. L. Affective neuroscience of pleasure: reward in humans and animals. *Psychopharmacology*. 2008, no. 3, pp. 457–480.

PANICUCC, J., PROUTY, D. & COLLINSON, R. *Adventure Education: Theory and Applications.* Champaign, IL: Human Kinetics, 2007. ISBN 978-073-6061-797.

CSÍKSZENTMIHÁLYI, M. *Finding Flow: The Psychology of Engagement with Everyday Life.* 1.st ed., New York: Basic Books, 1997. ISBN 04-650-2411-4.

CSÍKSZENTMIHÁLYI, M. *Flow: The Psychology of Optimal Experience.* New York: HarperPerennial, 1991. ISBN 00-609-2043-2.

[73]

NITOBE, I. *Bushido: The Soul of Japan: A Classic Essay on Samurai Ethics.* 1st ed., Tokyo: Kodansha International, 2002. ISBN 47-700-2731-1.

[74]

KEELY, L.C. Why isn't growth making us happier? Utility on the hedonic treadmill. *Journal of Economic Behavior*. 2005, 57th ed., no. 3, pp. 333–355.

LYUBOMIRSKY, S., SHELDON, K. M. & SCHKADE, D. Pursuing happiness: The architecture of sustainable change. 2005, UC Riverside.

SHELDON, K. M. & LYUBOMIRSKY, S. Achieving sustainable gains in happiness: Change your actions, not your circumstances. *Journal of Happiness Studies*. 2006, 7th ed., no. 1, pp. 55–86.

PINK, D. H. *Drive: The Surprising Truth About What Motivates Us*. 1st ed., New York: Riverhead Books, 2011. ISBN 978-159-4484-803.

[75]

MARCHAND, W. R. et al. Neurobiology of mood disorders. *Hospital Physician*, 2005, 41st ed., no. 9, pp. 17.

[76]

AMANO, T., DUVARCI, S., POPA, D. & PARE, D. The fear circuit revisited: Contributions of the basal amygdala nuclei to conditioned fear. *Journal of Neuroscience*. 2011, 31st ed., no. 43, pp. 15481–15489.

DIAMANDIS, P. H. & KOTLER, S. *Abundance: The Future Is Better Than You Think*. 1st ed., New York: Free Press, 2012. ISBN 14-516-1421-7.

SHERMER, M. *The Believing Brain: From Ghosts and Gods to Politics and Conspiracies – How We Construct Beliefs and Reinforce Them as Truths*. St. Martin's Griffin, 2012. ISBN 978-125-0008-800.

[77]

AMANO, T., DUVARCI, S., POPA, D. & PARE, D. The fear circuit revisited: Contributions of the basal amygdala nuclei to conditioned fear. *Journal of Neuroscience*. 2011-10-26, 31st ed., no. 43, pp. 15481–15489.

DIAMANDIS, P. H. & KOTLER, S. *Abundance: The Future Is Better Than You Think*. 1st ed., New York: Free Press, 2012. ISBN 14-516-1421-7.

[78]

DIAMANDIS, P. H. & KOTLER, S. *Abundance: The Future Is Better Than You Think*. 1st ed., New York: Free Press, 2012. ISBN 14-516-1421-7.

SHERMER, M. *The Believing Brain: From Ghosts and Gods to Politics and Conspiracies – How We Construct Beliefs and Reinforce Them As Truths*. St. Martin's Griffin, 2012. ISBN 978-125-0008-800.

[79]

SWEENEY, P. D., ANDERSON, K. & BAILEY, S. Attributional style in depression: A meta-analytic review. *Journal of Personality and Social Psychology.* 1986, 50th ed., no. 5, pp. 974–991.

PETERSON, C., MAIER, S. F. & SELIGMAN, M. E. P. *Learned Helplessness: A Theory for the Age of Personal Control.* New York: Oxford Univ. Press, 1993. ISBN 978-019-5044-676.

SELIGMAN, M. E. P. *Learned Optimism: How to Change Your Mind and Your Life.* 1st ed., New York: Vintage Books, 2006. ISBN 140-007-8393-1400.

[80]

HAUB, C. How Many People Have Ever Lived on Earth? *Population Reference bureau* [online]. 1995, 2002 [qt. 2013-03-25]. Web: https://www.prb.org/howmanypeoplehaveeverlivedonearth/

[81]

The study mentioned was conducted initially with rats and electric shocks but for more poetical and simpler example we used the model with hamsters and boxes.

SELIGMAN, M. E. P. Learned helplessness. *Annual Review of Medicine.* 1972, 23rd ed., no. 1, pp. 407–412.

SELIGMAN, M. E., ROSELLINI, R. A. & KOZAK, M. J. Learned helplessness in the rat: Time course, immunization, and reversibility. *Journal of Comparative and Physiological Psychology*, 1975, 88th ed., no. 2, pp. 542–547.

SELIGMAN, M. E. *Helplessness: On Depression, Development, and Death.* New York: W. H. Freeman, 1992. ISBN 07-167-2328-X.

PETERSON, C., MAIER, S. F. & SELIGMAN, M. E. P. *Learned Helplessness: A Theory for the Age of Personal Control.* New York: Oxford Univ. Press, 1993. ISBN 978-019-5044-676.

SELIGMAN, M. E. P. *Learned Optimism: How to Change Your Mind and Your Life.* 1st ed., New York: Vintage Books, 2006. ISBN 140-007-8393-1400.

[82]

SELIGMAN, M. E., ROSELLINI, R. A. & KOZAK, M. J. Learned helplessness in the rat: Time course, immunization, and reversibility. *Journal of Comparative and Physiological Psychology*, 1975, 88th ed., no. 2, pp. 542–547.

[83]

ZIMBARDO, P. & BOYD, J. *The Time Paradox: The New Psychology of Time That Will Change Your Life.* 1st ed., New York: Free Press, 2009. ISBN 978-141-6541-998.

[84]

ZIMBARDO, P. G. & BOYD, J. N. Putting time in perspective: A valid, reliable individual-differences metric. *Journal of Personality and Social Psychology.* 1999, 77th ed., no. 6, pp. 1271–1288.

HARBER, K., ZIMBARDO, P. G. a BOYD, J. N. Participant self-selection biases as a function of individual differences in time perspective. *Basic and Applied Social Psychology.* 2003, 25th ed., no. 3, pp. 255–264.

ZIMBARDO, P. G. & BOYD, J. N. *The Time Paradox: The New Psychology of Time That Will Change Your Life.* 1st ed., New York: Free Press, 2009. ISBN 978-141-6541-998.

[85]

FRANKL, V. E. *Man's Search for Meaning.* Boston: Beacon Press, 2006. ISBN 08-070-1427-3.

[86]

BROWN, M. Comfort zone: Model or metaphor? *Australian Journal of Outdoor Education.* 2008, 12th ed., no. 1, pp. 3–12.

PANICUCC, J., PROUTY, D. & COLLINSON, R. *Adventure Education: Theory and Applications.* Champaign, IL: Human Kinetics, 2007. ISBN 978-073-6061-797.

[87]

TEDESCHI, R. G. & CALHOUN, L. G. Target article: Posttraumatic growth. *Psychological Inquiry.* 2004, 15th ed., no. 1, pp. 1–18.

SELIGMAN, M. E. P. *Flourish: A Visionary New Understanding of Happiness and Well-Being.* 1st ed., New York: Free Press, 2012. ISBN 978-143-9190-760.

[88]

PAUSCH, R. & ZASLOW, J. *The Last Lecture.* 1st ed., New York: Hyperion, 2008. ISBN 14-013-2325-1.

[89]

SELIGMAN, M. E. P., STEEN, T. A., PARK, N. & PETERSON, C. Positive psychology progress: Empirical validation of interventions. *American Psychologist*. 2005, 60th ed., no. 5, pp. 410–421.

U.S. ARMY. *Comprehensive Soldier & Family Fitness: Building Resilience & Enhancing Performance* [online]. 2013, [qt. 2013-03-25]. Web: http://ready.army.mil/ra_csf.htm

SELIGMAN, M. E. P. *Flourish: A Visionary New Understanding of Happiness and Well-Being.* 1st ed., New York: Free Press, 2012. ISBN 978-143-9190-760.

[90]

SELIGMAN, M. E. P., STEEN, T. A., PARK, N. & PETERSON, C. Positive psychology progress: Empirical validation of interventions. *American Psychologist*. 2005, 60th ed., no. 5, pp. 410–421.

SELIGMAN, M. E. P. *Flourish: A Visionary New Understanding of Happiness and Well-Being.* 1st ed., New York: Free Press, 2012. ISBN 978-143-9190-760.

[91]

KAHNEMAN, D. & KRUEGER, A. B. Developments in the measurement of subjective well-being. *Journal of Economic Perspectives*. 2006, 20th ed., no. 1, pp. 3–24.

SCHWARZ, N. & STRACK, F. Reports of subjective well-being: Judgmental processes and their methodological implications. *Well-being: The foundations of hedonic psychology*, 1999, pp. 61–84.

SCHWARZ, N. & CLORE, G. L. Mood, misattribution, and judgments of well-being: Informative and directive functions of affective states. *Journal of Personality & Social Psychology*. 1983, 45th ed., no. 3, pp. 513–523.

BOWER, G. H. Mood and memory. *American Psychologist*. 1981, 36th ed., no. 2, pp. 129–148.

WATKINS, P. C., VACHE, K., VERNEY, S. P. & MATHEWS, A. Unconscious mood-congruent memory bias in depression. *Journal of Abnormal Psychology*. 1996, 105th ed., no. 1, pp. 34–41.

GILBERT, D. T. *Stumbling on Happiness.* 1st ed., New York: A. A. Knopf, 2006. ISBN 14-000-4266-6.

[92]

FUOCO, M. A. Trial and error: They had larceny in their hearts, but little in their heads, *Pittsburgh Post-Gazette*, 1996-05-21.

KRUGER, J. & DUNNING, D. Unskilled and unaware of it: how difficulties in recognizing one's own incompetence lead to inflated self-assessments. *Psychology*, 2009, no. 1, pp. 30–46.

[93]

JOHNSON-LAIRD, P. N. *Mental Models: Towards a Cognitive Science of Language, Inference, and Consciousness.* 5th ed., Cambridge, Mass: Harvard University Press, 1993. ISBN 978-067-4568-822.

PRINCETON UNIVERSITY. *Mental Models & Reasoning* [online]. [qt. 2013-03-25]. Web: http://mentalmodels.princeton.edu

[94]

KRUGER, J. & DUNNING, D. Unskilled and unaware of it: how difficulties in recognizing one's own incompetence lead to inflated self-assessments. *Psychology*, 2009, no. 1, pp. 30–46.

[95]

HARRIS, S., SHETH, S. A. & COHEN, M. S. Functional neuroimaging of belief, disbelief, and uncertainty. *Annals of Neurology*. 2008, 63rd ed., no. 2, pp. 141–147.

[96]

VUILLEUMIER, P. Anosognosia: The neurology of beliefs and uncertainties. *Cortex*. 2004, 40th ed., no. 1, pp. 9–17.

VALLAR, G. & RONCHI, R. Anosognosia for motor and sensory deficits after unilateral brain damage: A review. *Restorative Neurology and Neuroscience*, 2006, 24th ed., no. 4, pp. 247–257.

PRIGATANO, G. P. & SCHACTER, D. L. *Awareness of Deficit after Brain Injury: Clinical and Theoretical Issues.* New York: Oxford University Press, 1991. ISBN 01-950-5941-7.

[97]

The anatomical basis of anosognosia – backgrounder. *Treatment Advocacy Center* [online]. 2012 [qt. 2013-03-25]. Web: http://www.treatmentadvocacycenter.org/key-issues/anosognosia

[98]

CRITCHLEY, M. Modes of reaction to central blindness. *Proceedings of the Australian Association of Neurologists*, 1968, 5th ed., no. 2, pp. 211.

PRIGATANO, G. P. & SCHACTER, D. L. *Awareness of Deficit after Brain Injury: Clinical and Theoretical Issues*. New York: Oxford University Press, 1991. ISBN 01-950-5941-7.

[99]

KRUGER, J. & DUNNING, D. Unskilled and unaware of it: How difficulties in recognizing one's own incompetence lead to inflated self-assessments. *Psychology*, 2009, no. 1, pp. 30–46.

[100]

ARIELY, D. *The Upside of Irrationality: The Unexpected Benefits of Defying Logic*. 1st ed., New York: HarperPerennial, 2011. ISBN 978-006-1995-040.

ARIELY, D. *Predictably Irrational: The Hidden Forces That Shape Our Decisions*. 1st ed., New York: Harper Perennial, 2010. ISBN 978-006-1353-246.

[101]

WHITSON, J. A. & GALINSKY, A. D. Lacking control increases illusory pattern perception. *Science*. 2008, 322nd ed., no. 5898, pp. 115–117.

MUSCH, J. & EHRENBERG, K. Probability misjudgment, cognitive ability, and belief in the paranormal. *British Journal of Psychology*. 2002, 93rd ed., no. 2, pp. 169–177.

BRUGGER, P., LANDIS, T. & REGARD, M. A "sheep-goat effect" in repetition avoidance: Extrasensory perception as an effect of subjective probability? *British Journal of Psychology*. 1990, 81st ed., no. 4, pp. 455–468.

SHERMER, M. *The Believing Brain: From Ghosts and Gods to Politics and Conspiracies – How We Construct Beliefs and Reinforce Them as Truths*. St. Martin's Griffin, 2012. ISBN 978-125-0008-800.

[102]

BBC. 1978: Mass suicide leaves 900 dead. *BBC.com* [online]. 1978-11-18 [qt. 2013-03-25]. Web: http://news.bbc.co.uk/onthisday/hi/dates/stories/november/18/newsid_2540000/2540209.stm

WESSINGER, C. *How the Millennium Comes Violently: From Jonestown to Heaven's Gate*. New York: Seven Bridges Press, 2000. ISBN 18-891-1924-5.

Acknowledgements

A huge thank-you goes to my whole team around the world. Without all of you, this book would not exist. To everyone at New Leaf Literary and St. Martin's Press, thank you for all the incredible work you've done to make this project happen.

And most importantly, to my parents and grandparents, thank you for your guidance and values, shaping me into the person I am today.

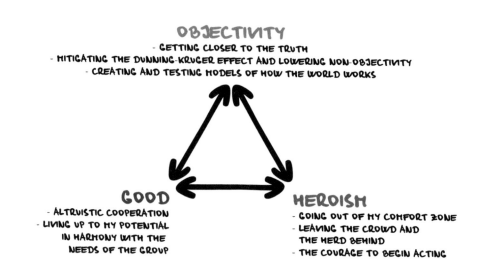

The good life is one inspired by love and guided by knowledge.

—Bertrand Russell